EASTERN EUROPE SINCE STALIN

EASTERN EUROPE SINCE STALIN

Compiled and Edited by

Jonathan Steele

CRANE, RUSSAK & COMPANY, INC.

NEW YORK

First published 1974 by
David & Charles (Holdings) Limited
South Devon House Newton Abbot Devon
ISBN 0 7153 6429 4

Published in the United States of America by
Crane, Russak & Company, Inc.
347 Madison Avenue, New York, N.Y. 10017
ISBN 0 8448 0273 5
Library of Congress Catalog Card
Number 73 91603

Printed in Great Britain

Contents

PAGE

INTRODUCTION   9

PART ONE: THE LEGACY OF STALIN   13

THE LAST YEARS   17
1   Marie Majerova. *Children of the Stalin era*   18
2   Georgi Malenkov. *Comrade Stalin, leader of
    progressive mankind*   20
3   Milovan Djilas. *Raptures*   21
4   Milan Kundera. *Why I became a communist*   24
5   A. J. Liehm. *An attempt at an answer*   25
6   Milovan Djilas. *Yugoslavia's break with Moscow*   28
7   *The Trial of Rudolf Slansky*   31

DE-STALINISATION BEGINS   33
8   *Pravda. Collective leadership*   33
9   Imre Nagy. *The new course in Hungary*   36
10 Georgi Malenkov. *The new course in the USSR*   39
11 Dimitri Shepilov. *Attack on the new course*   41
12 Nikita Khruschev. *An apology to Tito*   43
13 Nikita Khruschev. *Secret speech, 1956*   46

PART TWO: THE PEOPLE TAKE TO
THE STREETS   54
HUNGARY 1956   56
14   Judith Mariassy. *Unpleasant questions*   56
15   Antal Apro. *The burial of Laszlo Rajk*   58
16   Petöfi Circle. *The writers' demands*   62
17   *The students' demands*   63
18   Radio Kossuth. *The election of workers' councils*   66
19   Edward Kardelj. *Socialism must develop*   69

POLAND 1956   72
20   Leszek Kolakowski. *Marx needs to be resurrected*   73
21   Wladyslaw Gomulka. *The Polish model of socialism*   76
22   Stefan Kisielewski. *Hangover or the general impotence*   81
23   Stefan Kisielewski. *Conventional language*   82

PART THREE: NATIONAL COMMUNISM   84
YUGOSLAVIA'S INDEPENDENT LINE   87
24   *The Moscow declaration, 1957*   89
25   *Kommunist. Moscow's criticism of Yugoslavia*   93

ALBANIA AND CHINA BREAK AWAY   99
26   Enver Hoxha. *Albania denounces Khruschev*   102
27   Nikita Khruschev. *Attack on the Albanians*   108
28   Chou En-Lai. *A rebuke for Khruschev*   113
29   *The Chinese letter*   114

RUMANIA OPPOSES COMECON   119
30   Nikita Khruschev. *On supranational planning*   121
31   Rumanian Communist Party. *Rumania's declaration
     of independence*   125

PART FOUR: THE QUIET YEARS AND THEIR SUDDEN END 128

ATTEMPTS AT REFORM 129

32 Evsei Liberman. *Profits in the Soviet Union* 130

33 Rezsoe Nyers. *Hungary's slow advance* 134

34 Ota Sik. *The legacy of central planning* 136

35 Alexander Solzhenitsyn. *Stalin's labour camps exposed* 139

36 Yuli Daniel. *Final plea* 142

37 P. G. Grigorenko. *On Tatar rights* 146

POLAND 1968 148

38 Jacek Kuron and Karol Modzelewski. *The rule of the bureaucracy* 149

39 Wladyslaw Gomulka. *On the Jews* 153

40 Andrzej Werblan. *Why are there so many Jews?* 155

CZECHOSLOVAKIA 1968 157

41 Gustav Husak. *Propaganda and analysis are not the same* 159

42 Czechoslovak Communist Party. *Action programme* 161

43 Ludvik Vaculik. *The two thousand words* 165

44 Alexander Dubcek. *Address to the nation* 172

45 *Appeal against the invasion* 176

46 *Student. An appeal to all students of the world* 177

47 *Pravda. The Brezhnev doctrine* 178

48 Leonid Brezhnev. *On 'subversion'* 181

49 *The Chronicle of Current Events. Soviet protest* 184

PART FIVE: THE CONSUMER REVOLUTION 187

50   Polish Workers. *Confrontation with Edward Gierek*   191

51   Leonid Brezhnev. *The switch to consumer goods*   195

52   Janos Kadar. *Life is a compromise*   197

53   Edit Fel and Tamas Hofer. *The change in peasant life*   201

54   W. Adamski. *Young people—1971*   205

     EPILOGUE   207

     SUGGESTIONS FOR FURTHER READING   209

     ACKNOWLEDGEMENTS   212

     INDEX   213

Introduction

It is just 21 years since the Soviet party and Government authorities announced in Moscow that 'the heart of our wise leader and teacher, J. V. Stalin, has ceased to beat'. They went on to promise to prevent 'any kind of panic'.

The promise was unnecessary. Panic was not the emotion with which most people greeted the news. Even in official Communist party circles, in the 'people's democracies' as well as in the Soviet Union, it took only 3 years for Stalin's image to be shattered. In 1956 at a closed session of the Twentieth Party Congress from which foreign Communist delegates were excluded Khruschev made a formidable attack on Stalin, on his 'cult of personality', on the terroristic methods of his purges, on the sycophancy of his subordinates, and on his violation of Lenin's death-bed wishes. With that speech de-Stalinisation took on a new momentum.

It is no accident that even now 21 years after Stalin's death de-Stalinisation is still the commonest shorthand expression used to describe the trend of the past two decades. Even though the image of Stalin as benevolent father-figure soon died, the stamp of his rule was so deep that it has needed years for it to be effaced.

The process of de-Stalinisation has gone in fits and starts. Throughout Eastern Europe it has been a case of two steps forward and one step back. The first rush to change the system brought subsequent retreats, in the Soviet Union in 1955, and then in Poland and Hungary in 1956. The pace of de-Stalinisation varied from country to country. It took until 1968 for the full force of it to reach Czechoslovakia. De-Stalinisation is a broad concept. It includes the abolition of arbitrary police powers, the rehabilitation of the victims of the purges, decentralisation in the economy, a shift away from heavy industry towards more production of consumer goods, and the recognition of a role for the non-party citizen in society. All these features now obtain to a greater or lesser extent in Eastern Europe. They are probably irreversible.

Only in connection with the Soviet Union itself has there been any talk of re-Stalinisation, and even there the word is an emotive phrase rather than an accurate description of events. A return to Stalin's system is inconceivable.

Outside the Soviet Union in the rest of Eastern Europe de-Stalinisation has gone further. It always was a different phenomenon. Whereas in the Soviet Union de-Stalinisation was a matter of internal reform, elsewhere it had important foreign policy connotations. It meant the breaking-down of the Soviet Union's rigid control over every aspect of life in the other East European states. It meant a recognition by Moscow that the building of socialism must take account of different conditions in different countries. It meant acceptance of private agriculture in Poland, or the survival of a substantial sector of private industry in East Germany. It meant a new chance for local and national self-expression. Above all, it meant qualified independence of, and not slavish subservience to, Moscow. The history of the last two decades in Eastern Europe is the story of the rise of national Communism.

De-Stalinisation has been more dramatic outside the Soviet Union for a second reason. In the USSR Stalin ruled for 25 of the first 35 years since the October Revolution. For all his mistakes, distortions, and crimes he nevertheless built up the country, industrialised it, and made it into a world power. The two decades since his death must be seen against the background of this long evolution. They could not make a sudden alteration in the course of history.

In the 'people's democracies' however Stalin ruled for from 5 to 8 years. He imposed his pattern in a hurry, clumsily, and largely by force. His death was the opportunity for urgent change. Although in the event de-Stalinisation was not a smooth or short process because of popular impatience and Soviet resistance, it was and had to be a dramatic alteration and in some cases a reversal of previous policies. The tensions inherent in Stalinism were greater in the 'people's democracies' than in the Soviet Union. The tensions of de-Stalinisation were consequently greater too.

For this reason this study makes no apology for devoting so much emphasis to the 'people's democracies'. Their hectic relations with the Soviet Union have been a major feature of the last 20 years. They have also changed more rapidly than the Soviet Union. What kind of societies have they now become? What is it like, this forgotten half of the European continent, which is so often overlooked by those who talk in Brussels of the New Europe, the Europe of the Nine, or just 'Europe', as though east of the Elbe nothing existed? If the major part of this book is an historical account of the changes since Stalin died, it is only right that it should end with some evidence of the 'normality' and 'ordinariness' of life in Eastern Europe now. Totalitarianism is no longer much use as a concept in analysing Eastern Europe. Authoritarian or centralised welfare states is a better description.

Finally, a word about the documents themselves. With the exception of half a dozen items, every text was published originally in Eastern Europe. In view of the controlled nature of the press and publishing houses there reprinting only such texts was a difficult decision to take. But to have included items from outside Eastern Europe, the eyewitness impressions for example of Western visitors, the memoirs of diplomats, or newspaper articles by Western correspondents, would have opened the door to a mass of material whose selection would have posed other problems of interpretations, analysis and bias. In fact, as the collection of documents will I hope show, the political ups-and-downs and about-turns in the past two decades in Eastern Europe have produced plenty of controversy and numerous eye-opening speeches and articles. In a few cases I have also included texts which originated in Eastern Europe but were unpublished 'underground' material until they became available in the West—transcripts of trials, petitions and appeals. They make important additions to our understanding of the area, and deserve to be included.

PART ONE

The Legacy of Stalin

Stalin died on 5 March 1953. He left behind him a country whose top political leaders were filled with fear of him and suspicion of each other. In virtually every country in the rest of Eastern Europe a series of purge trials had begun which were to bring about the execution and imprisonment of many of the most devoted Communist leaders of the generation which had fought Fascism and Nazism.

His economic testament was an article published in Pravda *6 months before he died, entitled 'The economic problems of socialism in the USSR'. Its main message was that economic development must be based on the fastest possible growth of heavy industry and the denial of any material incentives to the peasantry to raise food production. The policy was being all too slavishly adopted.*

Abroad, Stalin bequeathed his heirs an empire in Eastern Europe in which the Soviet Union controlled all political developments, quartered its troops, and exploited the economic resources by means of so-called joint companies in which the Soviet Union had the decisive voice. Yugoslavia was the only country which had managed to break loose from this system. As a result Stalin claimed to see Titoist agents or 'national deviationists', their ideological equivalents, under every bed. His determination to achieve total control from Moscow was only strengthened.

With his death it was only a matter of time before the edifice began to subside. It started almost at once. Partly for fear of letting a clear successor emerge and partly out of genuine revulsion from the system of one-man dictatorship the survivors in the Kremlin set up a 'collective leadership'. Within a month they had announced an amnesty for thousands of prisoners, important price reductions, and the rehabilitation and release of the fifteen Kremlin doctors who had been arrested during the dictator's last days for allegedly plotting to murder Stalin and other top leaders.

In July the central committee announced that Lavrenti Beria, Stalin's Chief of Internal Affairs, had been dismissed and arrested. In December it was disclosed that he had been sentenced at a secret trial and executed.

A collective leadership did not mean a united leadership. Two schools of thought emerged. One was led by Georgi Malenkov, the new Chairman of the Council of Ministers, and to a lesser extent by Nikita Khruschev, one of the five members of the secretariat of the central committee. They wanted substantial economic reforms and some relaxation of political life. A more conservative group which wanted only minor alterations in the Stalinist system was formed by Vyacheslav Molotov, for 30 years one of Stalin's most trusted collaborators, and by Lazar Kaganovich.

The decisive events for the reformist group were sudden and unexpected upheavals in Czechoslovakia and East Germany. At the end of May 1953 the Czechoslovak leadership announced a drastic monetary reform which abolished all savings accounts from before 1945 and obliged people to change their money into new currency at a minimum ratio of five old crowns to one new one. The idea was to control the inflation which followed the ending of food rationing by soaking up excess purchasing power. For thousands of people the change meant an immediate drop in living standards. Workers rioted in the industrial cities of Ostrava and Pilsen.

Two weeks later in East Germany there were more serious riots. Here Walter Ulbricht, the East German party leader, had deliberately rejected suggestions from Moscow that he loosen up. Instead, he had gone ahead with an announcement that workers' output norms be raised by 10 per cent. In East Berlin and several other parts of the country workers rebelled.

These double working-class disturbances produced an immediate push for reform. In East Germany the increase in output norms was rescinded. In Moscow in August Malenkov launched a new economic course. From then on living standards were to be increased dramatically and the emphasis of the economic plans was to be shifted from heavy industry to consumer goods. When it came to dealing with the peasants, no such clear line was laid down. But the general relaxation implied that the trend towards rapid and complete collectivisation of agriculture ought to be slowed down. In Poland the leadership assured peasants that individual farming would continue 'for a long time to come'. In Czechoslovakia and Hungary they were told they could abandon the collective farms and go back to individual farming.

The most dramatic example of the 'new course' came in Hungary. Immediately after the East German events the Soviet leaders summoned the Hungarian party chiefs to Moscow and ordered them to change their policy. The post of Prime Minister was given to Imre Nagy, who had been dismissed in 1949 for opposing what he considered to be the excessively severe and hasty collectivisation drive. Nagy was now authorised to announce far-reaching political and economic reforms.

The establishment of collective leadership in Moscow brought similar modifications of one man rule in the 'people's democracies'. The old Stalinist rulers were obliged to delegate some of their power. They had to split the Prime Minister's job from that of the first party secretary, and divest themselves of one of them.

But the move was resisted in the spirit, and in some cases in the letter. Only in Czechoslovakia, where President Gottwald died soon after catching pneumonia at Stalin's funeral, was there a vacuum at the top. Elsewhere Stalin's appointees were not ready to abandon their conservatism in a hurry. Nor was the Kremlin ready to abandon them entirely. Although some of the new Soviet leaders might have been glad to see the end of men like the East German leader, Walter Ulbricht, or Matyas Rakosi in Hungary or Poland's Boleslaw Bierut, it was feared that the notion of toppling them altogether might be too unsettling.

In Czechoslovakia and Hungary the top state and party jobs were split off immediately. In Bulgaria and Rumania the process was slower. There the old leaders Velko Chervenkov and Gheorghe Gheorghiu-Dej held on to the combined top party and Government post for another year.

The compulsory division of functions coincided with a division of opinion in the party leadership. Just as in Moscow, reformers and conservatives differed over how far de-Stalinisation ought to go. The objective conditions were different in the 'people's democracies', since an important factor in de-Stalinisation there was the need to loosen the Kremlin's monolithic control, and achieve greater latitude for reformist local leaderships to take account of specific national and local conditions in each country. The seeds of the later debate on 'different roads to socialism' were already growing. The Soviet model could not be imported wholesale into the rest of Eastern Europe.

For their part the old Stalinist leaders were also conscious of this national dimension in de-Stalinisation, and of its potentially explosive power. They could and did use the argument with Moscow that too rapid a change in countries where the 'construction of socialism' was less than a decade old could create instability.

In Czechoslovakia and Hungary conservatives fought hard to water down the reforms. Agriculture was the issue on which they chose to resist most tenaciously. A miniature version of the great debate over collec- tivisation of agriculture, which had split the Soviet leadership in the late 1920s, broke out in Eastern Europe. The reformers argued that forced collectivisation led to a drop in food production, and that in the still relatively early stages of the building of socialism it was foolish to alienate the peasantry. The conservatives replied that small peasant holdings could never bring about a sustained and long-range increase in production. Collectivisation would have to come sooner or later. The sooner, they said, the better.

Under Stalin the degree of collectivisation in each country had been patchy. By the end of 1953 collectives covered 40 per cent of the agricultural area in Czechoslovakia and only 8 per cent in Poland. In Hungary approximately a quarter of the area was in collective farms.

After Stalin's death the reformers temporarily won the argument while collectivisation was halted. But the debate rumbled on until 1955, when Malenkov's 'New Course' was defeated in Moscow. A centrist leadership under Nikita Khruschev emerged. The switch away from heavy industry towards consumer goods was partially reversed. In Hungary Imre Nagy was replaced. In Czechoslovakia there was a move back towards collectivisation.

In spite of his centrist position on economic policy Khruschev soon proved to be far from conservative in foreign affairs, and on the need for internal political reform. He settled the long quarrel with Yugoslavia by going to Belgrade and apologising to President Tito. He accepted the notion that each country had to adapt its policies to specific local conditions. This was an event of decisive importance.

The psychological impact it caused was, however, as nothing to the stunned reaction which greeted Khruschev's speech at the Twentieth Congress of the Soviet party in February 1956. The Soviet leader accused Stalin, dead less than 3 years, of 'arrests and deportations on a mass scale', of executions without trial or explanation, and of authorising the murder of 'several thousand honest and innocent Communists'. He exploded the myth of Stalin's role in World War II, charging him with leaving the Soviet Union unprepared for the German invasion in 1941 in spite of several warnings. He attacked Stalin's policy towards Yugoslavia, for which he said the Sovet Union had 'paid dearly'.

The speech caused a sensation throughout the Communist world. Although it was made to a closed session of the Congress, from which all but the Russian delegates were excluded, its contents soon leaked out. De-Stalinisation had not only been sanctioned by the top leadership in the Kremlin. It was being taken further than anyone had dreamed possible. The prospects for change in Eastern Europe began to seem almost limitless. The hesitations and compromises which had marked the first phase of the reforms after Stalin's death now seemed to be over.

THE LAST YEARS

'The personality cult' has become so common a phrase that it is often forgotten how much of a cult it really was. In his last years Stalin was worshipped by the faithful in almost Messianic terms. For two or three days after his death the main party newspapers throughout Eastern Europe were given over almost entirely to fulsome tributes to him. This short essay came from the official daily newspaper of the Czechoslovak Communist Party, Rude Pravo.

B

1 Marie Majerova
CHILDREN OF THE STALIN ERA

Little Peter came home from school with a worried look. 'What's wrong? Have you got a pain?'

Peter replied gravely: 'Comrade Stalin is ill.'

Even his toys failed to interest him. He kept turning to his mother: 'Is Comrade Stalin badly ill? Has he got a doctor? Will he get better soon?'

The little chap was voicing the fears of all children of the Stalin era. All of them, from six-year-olds to teenagers, have been anxiously aware in the past few days that something extremely serious was happening. Their faces grew taut with the effort of grasping this terrible, portentous, shattering event.

Their eyes sank deep at the sight of the unheard-of danger. Their thoughts strayed as they returned continually to the same, one thing. The children were possessed, as were we all, by gnawing tension which drained one of all emotion. But they were also filled with faith and hope that the great Stalin would recover and that once again on May Day his arms would raise them to him over the balcony of the mausoleum so that they might behold their own wonderful future in the millionfold joy of the crowds. All our children, for whom the May Day scene was so familiar, and indeed the children of working people throughout the world saw themselves in the role of those two Young Pioneers* being raised up in Stalin's arms and lovingly protected.

The children of the Stalin era stood aghast and half-uncomprehending before the fact which had suddenly presented itself like a tragic historical monument. Stalin did not recover. The great man died. But day by day, as thoughts unfold and comprehension ripens, the children are coming to realise increasingly clearly what Stalin and his brilliant achievements mean for them.

* The Young Pioneers were members of the youth movement which included children from primary school age to teenage.

He it was who gave them their happy childhood in the joyful camps beside blue seas and among green mountains. He it was who in the Young Pioneer houses taught them that work is a pleasure and instructed them in the positive content of life.

He it was who began to bring about that the immense and previously unbelievable transformation of the world from the starvation of slavery in villages to which no paths led and where children perished by the thousand, from the tyranny of wild nature to a world of machine-tilled fields providing bread, to a world of exquisite cities, to a world where Man rules over nature—Man of the Stalin era—and shapes it for the well-being and happiness of future generations.

The lucky children who have lived in Stalin's time will bear this fact like a golden emblem throughout their lives. How those yet to be born will envy them! But the fact of having lived during Stalin's lifetime places upon every child the obligation to learn diligently all about Stalin's ideas and to carry out Stalin's well-laid plans with enthusiasm.

The task of the Stalin children as they step forth today into their era with a newly-acquired maturity—an era which Stalin clearly envisaged and marked out—is to set their course on its lines and to enter on the path of peaceful construction, on the path of Communism.

SOURCE: *Rude Pravo* (9 March 1953), written by Marie Majerova

On the occasion of Stalin's seventieth birthday on 21 December 1949
Pravda *ran to twelve pages instead of the usual four. Every line of the twelve pages, apart from a 2in theatre programme and a 3in report of a chess tournament, was given over to praising Stalin. Several Politburo members wrote articles, including Georgi Malenkov, excerpts of whose contribution appear here. His theme was a justification of the concept of the purge, and a call for Bolsheviks to practise self-criticism.*

2 Georgi Malenkov
COMRADE STALIN, LEADER OF PROGRESSIVE
MANKIND

The whole world has seen Stalin's greatness at major turning points of history—in October 1917 and during the Civil War and the intervention, when he and Lenin led the socialist revolution and the cause of defeating our motherland's powerful foes. . . .

When Fascism's dark forces loomed over the world during the Second World War, threatening the downfall of Man's culture, Comrade Stalin, heading the Soviet Union, directly guided the work of defeating Hitler's hordes. He ensured victory for the peace-loving nations and was the acknowledged leader of the hard struggle to free mankind from the oppression of Fascism.

When the Second World War ended and the new claimants to global domination appeared on the political horizon, Comrade Stalin called upon the peoples for a resolute struggle against the instigators of a new World War. He united the supporters of peace in a mighty force . . .

Comrade Stalin teaches us that we cannot advance without self-criticism, that it is as necessary to us as air and water, that essentially the strength of Bolshevism is that it does not fear self-criticism and draws energy for its further progress from criticism of its own shortcomings . . .

An unsatisfactory state of affairs in respect to self-criticism inevitably engenders among some executives a bureaucratic attitude, conceit, arrogance and boastfulness. . . . Such ills are cured primarily by the Party masses checking their leaders. Comrade Stalin teaches that check-up from above must be combined with check-up from below . . .

Comrade Stalin teaches that it is necessary to wage an unrelenting struggle against suppression of self-criticism and persecution for it. To persecute people for self-criticism, says

Comrade Stalin, means to kill all independent activity on the part of the Party organisation, to undermine the leaders' authority among the Party masses, to demoralise the Party and to permeate the life of the Party organisation with the anti-Party habits of bureaucrats, the sworn enemies of the Party.

Comrade Stalin trains our Party cadres in intolerance of boastfulness and complacency. He says that a Party leader does not dare to embellish reality or to conceal from the Party the true state of affairs. . . . Comrade Stalin constantly warns that not conceit, but modesty adorns a Bolshevik, that any leader, whatever his post is a servant of the people . . .

SOURCE: 'Current Soviet Policies: a documentary record of the Nineteenth Congress of the Communist Party of the Soviet Union and the reorganisation after Stalin's death', from *The Current Digest of the Soviet Press*, edited by Leo Gruliow, New York (1953). Translation Copyright 1973 by *The Current Digest of the Soviet Press*, published weekly at the Ohio State University by the American Association for the Advancement of Slavic Studies; reprinted by permission of the *Digest*

Milovan Djilas, vice-president of Yugoslavia and one of Tito's closest colleagues until 1954, was expelled from the League of Communists of Yugoslavia for criticising what he saw as the rise of 'a new class' made up of party bureaucrats. In a chapter entitled 'Raptures' in his book Conversations with Stalin *he recalled how during the wartime partisan struggle even the independent-minded Yugoslav Communists had succumbed to the personality cult.*

3 Milovan Djilas
RAPTURES

The Yugoslav Communist Party was not only as ideologically unified as the Soviet, but faithfulness to Soviet leadership was one of the essential elements of its development and its activity. Stalin was not only the undisputed leader of genius, he was the incarnation of the very idea and dream of the new society. This idolatry of Stalin's personality, as well as of more or less everything in the Soviet Union, acquired irrational forms and proportions. Every action of the Soviet Government—for example, the attack on Finland—and every unpleasant feature in the Soviet Union—for example, the trials and the purges—was defended and justified. What appears even stranger, Communists succeeded in convincing themselves that such actions were right and proper and in banishing the unpleasant facts from their minds.

Among us Communists there were men with a developed aesthetic sense and a considerable acquaintance with literature and philosophy, and yet we waxed enthusiastic not only over Stalin's views but also over the 'perfection' of the way he formulated them. I myself referred many times in discussions to the crystal clarity of his style, the penetration of his logic, and the aptness of his commentaries, as though they were expressions of the most exalted wisdom. But it would not have been difficult for me, even then, to detect that the style of any other author who wrote in the same way was drab, meagre, and an unblended jumble of vulgar journalism and the Bible. Sometimes the idolatry acquired ridiculous proportions: we seriously believed that the war would end in 1942, because Stalin said so, and when this failed to happen the prophecy was forgotten—and the prophet lost none of his superhuman power.

Source: *Conversations with Stalin* by Milovan Djilas, published by Rupert Hart-Davis, and in the USA by Harcourt Brace Jovanovich, Inc. © 1962 by Harcourt Brace Jovanovich, Inc. and reprinted with their permission

In retrospect the cult of Stalin seems ridiculous and depressing. It was an absurd perversion of socialism which led people at best to suspend all their rational and critical instincts in favour of a blind idolatry, and at worst was a mask for fear, flattery, and insecurity.

But it is important to remember the honest socialist idealism out oj which it grew and which alone makes it intelligible. When World War

II ended, vast numbers of people in Eastern Europe as in Western Europe felt that the moment for socialism in one form or another had arrived.

Although detailed measures were bound to differ from country to country, a movement towards the nationalisation of some, if not all, of the commanding heights of the economy and towards a welfare state was as marked in Britain as in Poland or Czechoslovakia. It is inaccurate to see Communist rule in Eastern Europe as an alien system imposed by Soviet tanks. In its early stages it was built up gradually on the foundations of socialist longings among sizeable sections of the local populations. The break-up of the landed estates, and the nationalisation of the largest enterprises, many of which had been in foreign hands before the war, were widely supported.

Nowhere was this more true than in Czechoslovakia. Before the war Czechoslovakia had a more democratic system of government than any other East European state. At its first postwar elections, held on 26 May 1946, all eight parties were committed to some form of nationalisation, and the expropriation of the agricultural estates. The Communist Party emerged from the general elections as the strongest party in the country. In Bohemia and Moravia it won 40·1 per cent of the vote. Its nearest rival, President Benes' Social-Nationalists, won 23·6 per cent and the Christian Democrats had 20·4 per cent. In Slovakia, with its mainly Catholic and rural population, the Christian Democrats won 61·4 per cent and the Communists were second with 30·5 per cent. But the combined results gave the Communists approximately 600,000 votes more than their nearest rival, the Christian Democrats.

Two years later the Communists and the leftwing Social Democrats combined in a bloodless coup to start closing down all organised opposition. They had the support of most of the country's working class and a substantial portion of the young intelligentsia. By that time on an international plane the cold war had started. President Truman had launched his 'doctrine' of 'containing Communism' in 1947. The Italian and French coalition Governments had dropped their Communist Ministers. The United States still had a monopoly of the atom bomb. For its part in 1947 the Soviet Union had activated the Cominform, a tightly knit grouping of the Communist parties of Eastern and Western Europe. In November 1947 the Cominform issued its own mirror image of the Truman Doctrine, polarising the international situation into a global struggle between 'American expansionism' and the 'forces of democracy'.

In this atmosphere the Czechoslovak coup was over-simplistically interpreted in the West as analogous to Czechoslovakia's submission to Nazi aggression 10 years earlier. The fact that there were no Soviet troops in the country and that the coup had considerable support tended to be overlooked. It was later on, with the onset of the purges and the other distortions brought on by Stalinism, that much of that support evaporated.

Milan Kundera was one of the wittiest and most brilliant of the Czech writers who began to beat at the walls of censorship in the mid-1960s. In this passage from his novel The Joke, *which is clearly autobiographical in parts, he describes why the hero had become a Communist as a student in the late 1940s.*

4 Milan Kundera
WHY I BECAME A COMMUNIST

I could have gone before various commissions and trotted out dozens of reasons why I had become a Communist, but the thing that had attracted, even infatuated me about the Communist movement was the feeling, however illusory, of being close to the helm of history. In those days we really were making big decisions about the fate of men and things—not least in the universities, where there were as yet few Communists among the professors so that in the initial years the Communist students ran the universities almost unaided, making the decisions on academic staffing, on teaching reform and on the curriculum. The elation we experienced is commonly called the intoxication of power, but, with a little goodwill, I could choose a rather less severe way of putting it: we were bewitched by history, intoxicated at having jumped on its back and being able to feel it beneath us. Admittedly, in most cases this did develop into an ugly lust for power, but all the same, just as all human dealings are ambivalent, there was at that time and with us youngsters in particular an altogether idealistic illusion that we were inaugurating a human era, an era when man—every man—would be neither outside history nor under the heel of history, but would direct and create it himself.

SOURCE: Reprinted from *The Joke* by Milan Kundera, translated from the Czech by David Hamblyn and Oliver Stallybrass, and published by Macdonald & Co (Publishers) Ltd (1969) and Penguin Books (1970)

De-Stalinisation came late to Czechoslovakia. When it began finally to be pushed in the mid-1960s, it was the country's writers who led the way. One of the most prevalent issues they had to explain to the younger generation brought up since the war was how they could have been so idealistic at the beginning. A generation made apathetic by the distortions of 15 years of centralised rule could not project themselves back to the original enthusiasm for the movement.

In an article published in May 1964 in Litcrarni Noviny, *the journal of the Czech Writers' Union, A. J. Liehm tried to explain. Though always committed, Liehm had a long history of nonconformity and rebellion. Born in Prague in 1924, he was one of the founders in 1945 of the weekly* Kulturni Politika, *which was closed for its unorthodox opinions in 1949. He later worked in the Czechoslovak Foreign Ministry for a time. Active during the reform movement of 1967 and 1968, he left the country after the Soviet-led invasion.*

5 A. J. Liehm
AN ATTEMPT AT AN ANSWER

To come to the point then: what were we like? In 1945 we were about as old as you are to-day. In contrast to you we had had two sets of experiences: the bourgeois republic, and the Nazi occupation. We knew bourgeois society not from foreign radio stations nor from books and magazines; we knew it from seeing its autopsy, internally and externally. And I assure you, its face was anything but pleasant, whatever angle you looked at it from. Munich led us to think about the political side of the matter, and the occupation strengthened our conviction finally that it is not enough merely to change appearances. The substance has to be changed too.

Our first encounter with Communism, with Lenin and with Marx during the darkness of the occupation was a revelation, the key to the door which we had been knocking at in our search for the way out of a world in which we had been born to a world which we wanted to create for ourselves and for you, for you whom we had then only just begun to think about. And next to this truth there appeared a tangible truth—Stalingrad, the Liberation, May Days. That all took place at a political level. Then there was our generation's wish to be associated with everything that the pre-war avantgarde had meant for us in the fields of culture, art, and sensibility; it became a religion for us, and we adopted it although for the most part we knew next to nothing of the controversies which had raged around it in those days which preceded our own.

We threw ourselves into the new era with all the elan, fervour, sincerity, and sectarianism of our twenty years— and, believe me, it was very similar to your elan, sincerity, and sectarianism, including that passion for discussion and that unwillingness to silence an opponent by any means other than by superior argument. It was an unwillingness which we inherited from the occupation just as you inherited it from the era of the cult of the personality. Stalin was a symbol for us but we knew nothing of Stalinism. At the time it did not affect us; it did not mark us. We learnt our socialism from Lenin, from Marx, and from Bukharin. On the one hand it was the rational answer to the reality of our short lives, on the other the ideal, but in no case was it the praxis. We knew nothing of deformed socialism. We had no inkling of it. . . .

SOURCE: *Literarni Noviny*, Prague

Two issues dominated Stalin's last years, and left wounds which were to fester throughout the next decade and a half. Any discussion of the period since his death would be incomplete without a backward look at them. One was Yugoslavia's break with Moscow. The other was the series of trials and purges which affected every one of the 'people's democracies'. The two were, of course, connected.

Once the Yugoslav rift had come, and Stalin saw that he could not cow President Tito back into line, his obvious fear was that the cancer of insubordination and successful imperialist intrigue, as he saw it, would spread. He suspected that there might be Titoist agents in the leadership of all the other parties. Each party was called to account. One way to show Stalin that they were taking effective action was to find a sacrificial victim in their midst.

In Hungary in 1949 the Foreign Minister, Laszlo Rajk, was executed for 'Titoism, treason, and espionage for the imperialists'. In Bulgaria Traicho Kostov, the party secretary, was executed for Titoism. In Rumania in 1952 Anna Pauker, a veteran Communist and member of the Politburo, was imprisoned. In Poland the party secretary, Wladyslaw Gomulka, was arrested in 1951 for 'nationalism' and for anti-Sovietism. In Czechoslovakia in 1952 the party secretary, Rudolf Slansky, was hanged.

In every country hundreds of other party and government officials were dismissed or imprisoned or both. In 1949, for example, Stalin's paranoia was such that the Soviet authorities in East Germany decreed that no one who had been a wartime emigré or a prisoner of war in the West or Yugoslavia could hold office.

The purges took on a momentum of their own. They were used by different factions in the party leadership to settle old scores. Often there was a three-way split, between those who had spent the war in Moscow, those who had been in the West and those who had remained at home in the underground or been shut in Nazi concentration camps. Rudolf Slansky, who was tried in Prague with ten others in the longest and most sensational trial of the period, had himself authorised the dismissal and imprisonment of lower-level officials before the security service turned round on him. He and many of his fellow accused were Jews who had been in exile in Moscow during the war. The trial had elements of an anti-Semitic vendetta.

Once started, the purges continued even after Stalin's death. In East Germany the purges affected fewer of the top leaders than in the other countries, but even there in May 1953 Franz Dahlem, one of Walter Ulbricht's closest rivals, was deprived of his party functions and accused of 'political blindness vis-a-vis the activities of imperialist agents'.

More than a year after Stalin died, Lucretius Patrascanu, one of the most eminent Rumanian Communist theoreticians, was tried and executed. In Bulgaria groups of 'imperialist agents' were being 'uncovered' and tried until the end of 1955.

On 28 June 1948 the Yugoslav Communist Party was expelled from the Cominform, the coordinating centre of the international Communist community. The move followed growing tension between Belgrade and Moscow over the activities of Soviet civilian and military advisers in Yugoslavia, whom the Yugoslavs accused of spying, and over Soviet accusations that pro-bourgeois elements were being tolerated in the Yugoslav leadership.

In essence, the argument was over Stalin's wish to control Yugoslavia's development as he saw fit rather than to accept that the Yugoslavs understood their own local situation best. Of all the countries in Eastern Europe Yugoslavia was the only one which had liberated itself without Soviet help and in which the national partisan struggle had been conducted almost entirely under Communist leadership. This gave Tito an unusually powerful base from which to resist Stalin's bullying.

In this extract from his book Conversations with Stalin, *Milovan Djilas describes a meeting in Moscow on 10 February 1948 which was a crucial landmark in the gradual split between the two countries. Stalin was angry that the Yugoslavs had agreed with the Bulgarians (who were represented at the meeting by Georgi Dimitrov) to sign a treaty, and with the Albanians to send troops to Albania.*

6 Milovan Djilas
YUGOSLAVIA'S BREAK WITH MOSCOW

At that moment the point of the meeting suddenly became clear, though no-one expressed it, namely that no relations between the 'people's democracies' were permissible that were

not in the interests and had not the approval of the Soviet
Government. It became evident that to the Soviet leaders, with
their great-power mentality (which was expressed in the concept of the Soviet Union as the 'leading force of socialism'),
and especially as they were always conscious that the Red Army
had liberated Rumania and Bulgaria, Dimitrov's statements
and Yugoslavia's obstinacy and lack of discipline were not only
heresy but a denial of the Soviet Union's 'sacred' rights.

Dimitrov tried to explain, to justify himself, but Stalin kept
interrupting without letting him finish. Here, at last, was the
real Stalin. His wit now turned into cruel malice and his aloof-
ness into intolerance. Still he kept restraining himself and
succeeded in keeping his temper. Without losing for a moment
his sense of the actual state of affairs, he upbraided the Bulgars
and bitterly reproached them, for he knew they would submit
to him, but in fact he had his sights fixed on the Yugoslavs—
as in the peasant proverb, 'She scolds her daughter in order to
reproach her daughter-in-law'.

Supported by Kardelj, Dimitrov pointed out that Yugoslavia and Bulgaria had not announced a signed treaty at Bled
but only a statement that an agreement had been reached
leading to a treaty.

'Yes, but you didn't consult us,' Stalin shouted. 'We learn
about your doings in the newspapers. You chatter like women
from the housetops whatever occurs to you, and then the news-
papermen get hold of it' . . .

Finally Kardelj was called upon to speak. He was red, and
as he usually did when he was excited, he hunched his head
down between his shoulders and made pauses in his sentences
where they did not belong. He pointed out that the treaty
between Yugoslavia and Bulgaria, signed at Bled, had been
previously submitted to the Soviet Government, but that the
Soviet Government had made no comment other than to
suggest that its duration should be 'twenty years' instead of
'for all time'.

Stalin kept glancing silently and not without reproach at

Molotov who hung his head and with clenched lips tacitly confirmed what Kardelj had said.

'Except for that suggestion, which we adopted,' Kardelj continued, 'there were no differences . . .'

Stalin interrupted him, no less angrily than he had interrupted Dimitrov. 'Nonsense! There are differences and grave ones. What do you say about Albania? You did not consult us at all about the entry of your army into Albania.'

Kardelj replied that we had the consent of the Albanian Government.

Stalin shouted, 'This could lead to serious international complications. Albania is an independent state. What do you think? Justification or no justification, the fact remains that you did not consult us about sending two divisions into Albania.'

Kardelj explained that none of this was yet final and added that he did not remember a single foreign problem about which the Yugoslav Government had not consulted the Soviet.

'It's not so,' Stalin cried. 'You don't consult us at all. That is not your mistake, but your policy—yes, your policy.'

SOURCE: *Conversations with Stalin* by Milovan Djilas, published by Rupert Hart-Davis, and in the USA by Harcourt Brace Jovanovich, Inc. © 1962 by Harcourt Brace Jovanovich, Inc. and reprinted with their permission

Rudolf Slansky had had an exemplary Communist career. He joined the Czechoslovak Communist Party in 1921. During the war he was in Moscow. In 1944 he returned to Slovakia and joined the partisans. After the liberation he became secretary-general of the party.

Then in 1951 he was arrested. Several months later on 20 November 1951 his trial opened in Prague. He was accused of being 'a Trotskyite, a Titoite, and a Zionist' and of working 'in the service of United States imperialism and under the direction of Western espionage centres and creating an anti-State conspiratorial centre in order to restore capitalism and drag Czechoslovakia into the imperialist camp'.

The most macabre aspect of the trial was the series of forced con-

fessions which he and the other defendants made after months of torture and psychological pressure. Slansky was found guilty and executed.

7 THE TRIAL OF RUDOLF SLANSKY

The afternoon session began with the examination of Slansky.
Presiding Judge: Accused Slansky, step before the microphone. Are you guilty of the four criminal acts of which you are accused?
Slansky: Yes.
Presiding Judge: The first crime is espionage.
Slansky: Yes.
Presiding Judge: High treason.
Slansky: Yes.
Presiding Judge: Sabotage.
Slansky: Yes.
Presiding Judge: Military treason.
Slansky: Yes.
Presiding Judge: Will you please tell us in what respect you admit your guilt?
Slansky (speaking slowly and haltingly, with a deep voice): I fully admit my guilt and I wish to describe in detail and truthfully everything I have done. I have done serious wrong so far as the interests of the Czechoslovak people are concerned. It is by right that I am judged by this court, by the people's democratic court, by right I am forced to answer to charges today before all the Czechoslovak people and also before all democratic peoples of the world. I shall therefore in my testimony spare neither myself nor my partners. Above all, I shall not spare myself, because I, as one of the most important officials of the Communist Party, misused this great trust vested in me by the Party and the Czechoslovak people, whose great achievements gained since 1945 I have threatened through my activities. First of all I wish to confess my guilt in that as an enemy of the Communist Party and the people's democratic regime I formed the anti-State conspiratorial centre at the

head of which I stood for several years—this centre of ours in which I concentrated a number of varied capitalist and bourgeois nationalist collaborators.

My collaborators became agents of imperialist espionage services, i.e. of the French, British, and in particular the US services; and carried out hostile activities serving the interests of the Anglo-US imperialists which aimed at liquidating the people's democratic order, restoring capitalism, and effecting a re-orientation of Czechoslovak foreign policy in favour of the Western capitalist powers. I carried out hostile activities within the Czechoslovak Communist party, in the economic, foreign, and security sectors . . .

Presiding Judge: How is it that you, who have been a member of the Czechoslovak Communist Party for thirty years, could become a servant of the imperialists and the organiser and leader of a conspiracy against the Czechoslovak people's democratic Republic?

Slansky replied that he had come from the bourgeois family of a rich merchant and this had influenced his personal traits and character. In 1921 he had joined the party, burdened with 'petty-bourgeois opinions which I never abandoned. This prevented me from becoming a real Communist. Therefore I did not act as a Communist and I did not fulfil honourably the duties arising from my membership of the Communist party. At the very beginning of my activities in the Communist party, I became guilty of small and gradually more serious opportunist deviations to the right and left, I moved away from the party line, I wavered and behaved like an opportunist. . . . The reason why I avoided exposure for so long was because I masked my hostile activities and acted politically in a two-faced manner. In public I played the part of a supporter of the party's Bolshevik line, while in reality I had abandoned the Bolshevik position . . .

SOURCE: *Sentenced and Tried: the Stalinist Purges in Czechoslovakia*, by Eugene Loebl, translated by Maurice Michael; published by Elek (1969). The transcript of the trial proceedings was prepared by the BBC Monitoring Service

DE-STALINISATION BEGINS

After Stalin's death the first tentative criticism of his methods came in a Pravda editorial 2 months later. Stalin's name was not mentioned and the excuse of 'wartime circumstances' was used to justify his tendency to apply 'administrative methods' rather than political leadership. Although implicit, the criticism was clear. The editorial praised the principle of collective leadership, which was soon to be adopted in the other countries of Eastern Europe too.

8 Pravda
COLLECTIVE LEADERSHIP

. . . The party committees are organs of political leadership. They cannot apply methods inherent in administrative-managerial agencies in their practical work. There were cases of this during the war. Wartime circumstances caused certain particular features in the methods of leadership which were to some extent justified for those conditions. But this led to serious shortcomings in the practical work of party organisations.

This is why in many very important cases of party work in the postwar period the party has set the task of raising the level of party leadership, of putting an end to such phenomena as the application in party organisations of administrative methods of leadership, which led to bureaucratisation of party work.

One of the fundamental principles of party leadership is collectivity in deciding all important problems of party work. It is impossible to provide genuine leadership if inner party democracy is violated in the party organisation, if genuine collective leadership and widely developed criticism and self-criticism are lacking. Collectiveness and the collegium principle represent a very great force in party leadership . . .

The principle of collectivity in work means, above all, that

c

decisions adopted by party committees on all cardinal questions are the fruit of collective discussion. No matter how experienced leaders may be, no matter what their knowledge and ability, they do not possess and they cannot replace the initiative and experience of a whole collective. In any collegium, in any directing collective, there are people who possess diverse experience, without relying upon which the leaders cannot make correct decisions and exercise qualified leadership.

Individual decisions are always or almost always one-sided decisions. Hence the very important requirement that decisions must rest on the experience of many, must be the fruit of collective effort. If this is not so, if decisions are adopted individually, serious errors can occur in work . . .

Leaders cannot consider criticism of themselves as a personal affront. They must be able to accept criticism courageously and show readiness to bend their will to the will of the collective. Without such courage, without the ability to overcome one's own vanity and to bend one's will to the will of the collective, there can be no collective leadership. . . .

For correct training of cadres it is important that they be placed under the supervision of the party masses, that officials display readiness not only to teach the masses but to learn from the masses as well. Collectivity in work is called upon to play an important role in this connection. Where the collective principle is violated the necessary conditions for criticism and self-criticism are absent, the sense of responsibility is blunted and officials are infected by dangerous conceit and smugness. It is precisely in such a situation that some workers begin to behave as if they know everything, as if only they can say anything which makes sense, and as if the role of others is only to support their opinion.

Such a situation prepares the ground for unprincipled, alien habits of kowtowing and flattery. There are cases in which the head of a party committee behaves incorrectly and the party committee members accept this and, in order not to mar relations with the committee head, tolerate unprincipled behaviour, do not think it necessary or possible to voice objections and even orient themselves to his views and defer to him in every-thing . . .

SOURCE: Slepov. 'Collectivity is the Highest Principle of Party Leadership', *Pravda* (16 April 1953); English translation in *The Current Digest of the Soviet Press*, V: 13 (9 May 1953). Translation Copyright 1973 by *The Current Digest of the Soviet Press*, published weekly at the Ohio State University by the American Association for the Advancement of Slavic Studies; reprinted by permission of the *Digest*

Unlike Czechoslovakia, postwar Hungary was still largely an agrarian country. Some 3 million Hungarians were landless farm labourers or owners of minute plots unable to support a family. In 1945 a land reform expropriated the large estates and redistributed them to peasants who were encouraged, but not forced, to join cooperatives.

A general election in that year resulted in 57 per cent of the votes going to the Smallholders' Party and roughly 17 per cent each to the Social Democrats and the Communists. In 1946 these two parties joined up with a fourth party, the National Peasant Party, to form a leftwing alliance. They persuaded the Smallholders to accept a programme nationalising the banks, the bauxite mines, the electric power companies and the five largest industrial enterprises.

But in the first months of 1947 the Smallholders' Party was gradually broken. Several of its MPs were arrested in connection with an alleged plot and its secretary-general, Bela Kovacs, was deported to the Soviet Union. Collectivisation of agriculture was now ready to start. A 5 year plan for forced industrialisation, launched in 1949, imposed heavy norms on miners and factory workers. For 4 years Hungary laboured under a period of the crudest Stalinism.

After Stalin's death the new Soviet leadership chose Hungary as the testing ground for the idea of reform, the so-called 'New Course'. Imre Nagy, a Communist, had been the first Minister of Agriculture after the war and was responsible for the popular land reform. A few months later he became Minister of the Interior but was soon replaced. He was put into the background and during the worst Stalinist phase had no high governmental or party responsibilities.

In June 1953 at the Soviet Union's insistence he was selected as Prime Minister. In this, his speech to Parliament on 4 July 1953, he outlined the new Government's programme of immediate reform.

9 Imre Nagy
THE NEW COURSE IN HUNGARY

... Turning to the problems of economic policy I wish to stress that the Government is following a policy based on the realistic goals and suggestions of the new directing principle of the Central Committee of the Hungarian Workers' Party. This means that in the course of the development of our national economy it will take into consideration the economic resources of our country, that it will not set goals which cannot be realised because we lack the necessary resources, whether it is raw materials or investments which are beyond the strength and productivity of our country, or other exaggerated tasks which would hurt the living standards of the population. In the field of economic policy the Government will keep in mind the old saying: stretch out only as far as your blanket reaches.

We cannot fail to see and report to our nation that the raised goals of the Five-Year plan are in many respects beyond our power. Their accomplishment takes up too much of our resources, hinders the growth of the material basis of welfare and has lately caused a drop in the standard of living. It is evident that substantial modification is needed in this field. The development of socialist heavy industry cannot be a purpose in itself . . .

We must re-direct our policy so as to slow down substantially the pace of progress in heavy industry and thereby place much greater stress than before on light industry, which produces consumer goods and food. By this means we must satisfy the growing needs of the population to an increasing degree . . .

The exaggerated farmers' co-operative movement undoubtedly

contributed to the unfavourable outcome of agricultural production, and the hasty pace at which we increased the number of co-operatives led to the inability of some of them to become economically strong for want of the necessary requirements. But the gravest consequence of the hasty progress of the farmers' co-operative movement was that the encroachments and violations of the voluntary principle caused serious disturbance among the working peasants, upset peaceful productive work, and led to the large-scale decrease of investments necessary for the improvement of farming. . . .

In order to secure the possibility of peaceful work for our working peasants and to dispel doubts about forcing the peasant farms into co-operatives, the Government considers it necessary and proper to slow down the co-operative movement and to insure adherence to the voluntary principle. It will enable those members of the farmers' co-operatives who wish to return to individual farming, because they hope to achieve prosperity that way, to quit the co-operatives at the end of the crop year. We will go even farther than that and will allow the liquidation of the co-operatives where a majority of the members request it. At the same time the Government will offer every help to the co-operatives in the future and will contribute loans and investments to improve their production and to help their members prosper, because we are convinced that this is the most practical road towards improving peasants' conditions. . . .

Other spheres of our economic life show the need for changes. During the past years the Government has expanded its activities in fields where individual initiative and enterprise still could play a great role towards meeting the needs of the population. These fields are the retail trade and small industry. Even though the craftsmen's co-operatives testify to a serious development, they cannot make up for the shortages in the field of small industry. This persuades the Government to make a place for private enterprise and to issue licences to those eligible according to the law . . .

In the activity of our judicial and police organs and our local councils, lawfulness, the basic principle of the State and Government of the people's democracy, has not prevailed . . . The large numbers of judicial proceedings in case of felonies and misdemeanours, the widely used administrative methods, the crop gatherings, the tax collection, the multitude of encroachments and abuses in the course of land regroupings and other pestering hurt the sense of justice of the population and shook its faith in the law, and loosened the ties between the working people and the state organs or local councils. Securing lawfulness is the most urgent task of the Government . . .

The institution of internment camps adds to the damage of legality. The fact that we did not satisfy the specification of the constitution of the people's republic and did not establish the institution of the State Prosecutor, which is the highest constitutional safeguard of law and order, undoubtedly played a great part in this.

Beginning in the spirit of forgiveness and in the interest of peace and radically remedying just complaints, the Government will introduce a Bill to Parliament releasing all prisoners whose crime is not serious enough to endanger the security of the state or the public by their release. At the same time it proposes to eliminate the institution of internment and close the concentration camps. In this way the Government wishes to enable those who have received public amnesty to return to their homes and families . . . Police justice is incompatible with the basic principles of democratic justice, which essentially means that the investigating organ itself brings judgement. The Government will abolish this remainder inherited from the old system.

SOURCE: *Szabad Nep* (5 July 1953), reprinted in *Hungarian Social Science Reader* (*1945–1963*), edited by Dr W. Juhasz (Munich 1965)

In the Soviet Union the New Course was less of a political reform than in Hungary. Political changes were to come later. But in the economic

*field the drive for industrialisation was slackened, and collective farm
peasants were freed to develop their own small private plots (described
in Malenkov's speech below as 'the personal subsidiary husbandry of
the collective farmer').*

*Speaking to the Supreme Soviet on 8 August 1953 Malenkov outlined
the new policies. They included a milder attitude to foreign affairs and
the promotion of peaceful co-existence.*

10 Georgi Malenkov
THE NEW COURSE IN THE SOVIET UNION

. . . The urgent task in the next two or three years is to secure,
by generally improving agriculture and further consolidating
the collective farms organisationally and economically, the
creation in our country of an abundance of food for the population and of raw materials for light industry . . .

In addition to providing a greater material incentive to
collective farmers to develop the common enterprises of their
collective farms, the Government and Central Committee of
the party have decided thoroughly to correct and revise the
wrong attitude which has arisen towards the personal subsidiary
husbandry of the collective farmer . . . Owing to defects in our
policy of taxation here, the collective farmer's income from his
personal subsidiary husbandry has diminished lately, and there
has also been a reduction in the amount of livestock, especially
cows, in the personal possession of the collective farmers, which
runs counter to party policy.

Accordingly, the Government and Central Committee deem
it necessary substantially to reduce the compulsory delivery
quotas levied on the personal subsidiary husbandry of the
farmers. They have decided to change the system of levying
the agricultural tax on collective farmers. The monetary tax
payable by them is to be reduced by an average of about a half,
and the arrears in agricultural taxes incurred in past years are
to be cancelled . . .

Desirous of promoting peaceful co-operation with all

countries, the Soviet Government attaches particular importance to strengthening the Soviet Union's relations with its
neighbours. To elevate these relations to the level of good-
neighbourliness is the aim for which we are striving and will
continue to strive . . .

The Soviet Union will consistently and firmly pursue a
policy of preserving and consolidating peace, will promote
co-operation and business relations with all states which have
a like desire, and strengthen the ties of brotherly friendship and
solidarity with the great Chinese people, and with all the
people's democracies.

We firmly stand by the belief that there are no disputed or
outstanding issues today which cannot be settled peacefully by
mutual agreement between the parties concerned.

This also relates to disputed issues between the United
States of America and the Soviet Union. We stand, as we have
always stood, for the peaceful co-existence of the two systems.
We hold that there are no objective reasons for clashes between
the United States of America and the Soviet Union. The
security of the two states and of the world, and the development
of trade between the United States of America and the Soviet
Union, can be ensured on the basis of normal relations between
the two countries . . .

SOURCE: Malenkov's Speech to the Supreme Soviet (8 August
1953). English translation in *Soviet News* (15 August 1953),
supplement

*The New Course was not welcomed by all the Soviet leadership. By the
beginning of 1955 a serious split had developed. In an article in* Pravda
*in January Dimitri Shepilov, a leading party theorist, criticised the
concentration on consumer goods. It was weakening the Soviet Union's
industrial and hence defence capacity, he argued.*

*A month later Malenkov admitted his 'guilt and responsibility' and
his 'insufficient experience', and resigned as Chairman of the Council of
Ministers. He was replaced by Marshal Nikolai Bulganin. The*

*collective leadership was now already effectively subordinated to the
authority of two men, Bulganin and Khruschev.*

11 Dimitri Shepilov
ATTACK ON THE NEW COURSE

Views utterly alien to Marxist-Leninist political economy and
to the general line of the Communist Party on some fundamental questions of development of the socialist economy have
begun to take shape of late among some economists and teachers
in our higher educational institutions . . .

They say that a preponderant development of the production
of the means of production, of heavy industry, has been an
economic necessity only, if you please, in the early stages of
the development of Soviet society when our country was
backward. But now that we have created a mighty industry,
the situation has changed radically. Production under socialism
is production for consumption. Faster production of the means
of production, of heavy industry (than of consumer goods)
contradicts the basic economic law of socialism, they say. Hence
the far-reaching conclusion: the policy, pursued by the party,
of forced development of branches of heavy industry has allegedly
entered into conflict with the basic economic law of socialism,
since forced development of branches of heavy industry retards
public consumption.

Grossly distorting the essence of party and Government
decisions to increase production of consumer goods, the authors
of this conception assert that since 1953 the Soviet Union has
entered a new stage of economic development, the essence of
which is allegedly a radical change in the party's economic
policy. While the party used to put the emphasis on developing
heavy industry, now, if you please, the centre of gravity has
shifted to developing light industry, to the production of
consumer goods. Trying to present their imaginary formulae as
requirements of the basic economic law of socialism, these
economists propose setting an identical rate of development for

heavy and light industry or even providing for the preponderant development of light industry as compared with heavy industry throughout the entire period of completing the building of socialism and the transition from socialism to communism.

If views of this kind were to become widespread, it would cause great harm to the entire cause of communist construction. It would lead to complete disorientation of our cadres on basic questions of the party's economic policy. In practice it would mean that development of our heavy industry, which is the backbone of the socialist economy, would take a descending line, leading to decline in all branches of the national economy, not a rise but a drop in the working people's living standards, to undermining the economic power of the Soviet land and its defence capacity.

SOURCE: Shepilov's 'The Party's general line and the vulgarisers of Marxism', *Pravda* (24 January 1955); English translation in *The Current Digest of the Soviet Press*, VI: 52 (9 February 1955). Translation Copyright 1973 by *The Current Digest of the Soviet Press*, published weekly at the Ohio State University by the American Association for the Advancement of Slavic Studies; reprinted by permission of the *Digest*.

Although Malenkov's New Course in the economy was partially abandoned, the relaxation in international affairs mentioned in Malenkov's speech of August 1953 (see Document 10) continued. In line with the principle of 'good-neighbourliness' enunciated then, it was apparent from mid-1954 onwards that Khruschev wanted to find a modus vivendi with Yugoslavia.

Stalin's handling of the rift with Tito, and his crude attempt to bring him into line by cutting off aid and trade to Yugoslavia, were seen as a major foreign policy error. A reconciliation with Tito would show that Moscow's desire for peace was genuine, and would remove the mistrust, fear, and suspicion which had pervaded the entire socialist camp as a result of the 'Titoist' purges. The purges had strengthened the hand of the old guard in the people's democracies and was preventing an effective break with Stalinism.

The idea of patching things up with Tito did not appeal to all Khruschev's colleagues in Moscow. Molotov for one severely criticised it. Mao Tse-Tung and the Albanians were sceptical—a foretaste of the major Sino-Soviet differences yet to come.

In May 1955 Khruschev flew with Bulganin to Belgrade for a meeting which culminated in an historic joint declaration. Its central core opened the way to pluralism within the Communist movement, or 'polycentrism' as the Italian party leader Palmiro Togliatti was to call it. The declaration praised the principle of 'mutual respect for, and non-interference in, internal affairs for any reason whatsoever, whether of an economic, political, or ideological nature, because questions of internal organisation, or difference in social systems, and of different forms of socialist development are solely the concern of the individual countries'.

As dramatic as this final declaration was Khruschev's opening statement at Belgrade airport on 26 May 1955. Stepping on to Yugoslav soil—itself a concession, since the Russians were coming to Tito and not vice versa—Khruschev apologised for the mistakes of the past and laid all the blame on the Soviet side.

12 Nikita Khruschev
AN APOLOGY TO TITO

Dear Comrade Tito, members of the Government and leaders of the Yugoslav Communist League, dear comrades and citizens:

In the name of the Presidium of the Supreme Soviet of the USSR, the Government of the USSR, and the central committee of the Communist party of the Soviet Union, and in the name of the Soviet people, I cordially greet you and the workers of the glorious capital of Yugoslavia, Belgrade, and all the brotherly peoples of Yugoslavia.

The Soviet delegation has come to your country to determine together with the Yugoslav Government delegation the roads of further development and consolidation of friendship and co-operation between our peoples, to consider our joint task in the struggle for prosperity, for reduction of tension, for strengthening peace in general and the security of peoples . . .

Our peoples will always remember that Yugoslav and Soviet soldiers joined forces in the battle for Belgrade, hit the enemy hard and liberated this ancient Slav city from the Hitlerite invaders. The peoples of the Soviet Union ardently welcomed the creation of the Federal People's Republic of Yugoslavia.

As we know, the best relations developed during those years between the peoples of the Soviet Union and Yugoslavia, between our States and parties. However, later these good relations were destroyed.

We sincerely regret what happened and resolutely reject the things that occurred, one after the other, during that period. On our part we ascribe without hesitation the aggravations to the provocative role that Beria, Abakumov*, and others— recently exposed enemies of the people—played in the relations between Yugoslavia and the USSR.

We studied assiduously the materials on which the serious accusations and offenses directed at that time against the leaders of Yugoslavia had been based. The facts showed that these materials were fabricated by enemies of the people, detestable agents of imperialism who by deceptive methods pushed their way into the ranks of our party.

We are profoundly convinced that this period of the deterioration of our relations has been left behind us. For our part we are ready to do everything necessary to eliminate all obstacles standing in the way of complete normalisation of relations between our states, of the consolidation of friendly relations between our peoples.

Today, when certain results have been achieved already in the field of normalising our relations, the Soviet delegation expresses the conviction that the forthcoming negotiations will lead to the development and consolidation of political, economic, and cultural co-operation among our peoples. All the conditions exist for such co-operation—centuries-old historic friendship between the peoples of our countries, the glorious

* Beria's deputy, sentenced and executed in 1954.

traditions of the revolutionary movement, the indispensable economic base and joint ideals in the struggle for peaceful advancement and the happiness of the working people.

Following the teachings of the creator of the Soviet state, Vladimir Ilyich Lenin, the Government of the Soviet Union bases its relations with other countries, large and small, on the principles of peaceful co-existence of states, on principles of equality, non-intervention and respect for sovereignty and national independence, on principles of non-aggression and recognition of the impermissibility of states' encroaching upon the territorial integrity of others.

We hope that the relations between our countries will continue to develop on these principles for the good of our peoples. This will be a new and important contribution to the cause of reduction of international tension, the cause of preservation and consolidation of general peace in the world.

SOURCE: Reprinted from *The Soviet-Yugoslav Controversy 1948 1958: a documentary record*, edited by Robert Bass and Elizabeth Marbury (New York 1959)

On 25 February 1956 Khruschev addressed a special session of the 20th party congress of the Soviet Communist Party. All foreign delegates were excluded. His speech was an astonishing attack on Stalin. At the end Khruschev even raised the dangerous question: 'Why did other Politburo members not assert themselves against the cult of personality?'

Although his reply amounted to a denial of his own or his colleagues' responsibility, the speech was the most penetrating official analysis of Stalinism that had yet been made. It was never equalled again. Khruschev's revelations about Lenin's so-called 'Testament', with its warning about Stalin, were also a sensation.

In the weeks after the Congress the speech was gradually made available to the leadership of other Communist parties. Its contents began to leak out, and on 4 June 1956 the United States Department of State released a text which had come into its hands. Its authenticity has not been refuted.

13 Nikita Khruschev
SECRET SPEECH, 1956

Comrades! In the central committee's report to the Twentieth Congress, in a number of speeches by delegates to the Congress, and also earlier during the plenary sessions, quite a lot has been said about the cult of the individual and about its harmful consequences.

After Stalin's death the central committee began to implement a policy of explaining concisely and consistently that it is impermissible and foreign to the spirit of Marxism-Leninism to elevate one person, to transform him into a superman with supernatural characteristics akin to those of a god. Such a man supposedly knows everything, thinks for everyone, can do anything, and is infallible in his behaviour.

Such a belief about a man, and specifically about Stalin, was cultivated among us for many years . . . We are concerned with a question which has immense importance for the party now and in the future—how did the cult of Stalin's personality gradually grow into the cult which became at a certain specific stage the source of a whole series of exceedingly serious and grave perversions of party principles, party democracy, and revolutionary legality?

Because not everybody yet realises fully the practical consequences of the cult of the individual, the great harm caused by the violation of the principle of collective leadership of the party and because of the accumulation of immense and limitless power in the hands of one person, the central committee considers it absolutely essential to make the relevant material available to the Twentieth Congress of the Communist Party of the Soviet Union . . .

The great modesty of the genius of the revolution, Vladimir Ilyich Lenin, is known. Lenin had always stressed the role of the people as the creator of history, the directing and organisational role of the party as a living and creative organism, and also the role of the central committee. Marxism does not negate the role of the leaders of the working class in directing the revolutionary liberation movement.

While ascribing great importance to the role of the leaders and organisers of the masses, Lenin at the same time mercilessly stigmatised every manifestation of the cult of the individual, inexorably countered unMarxist views about a 'hero' and a 'crowd' and countered all efforts to oppose a 'hero' to the masses and to the people . . .

Lenin's keen mind detected in time in Stalin those negative characteristics which resulted later in grave consequences. Fearing for the future fate of the party and of the Soviet nation, he pointed out that it was necessary to consider transferring Stalin from the position of Secretary-General because of Stalin's exceptional rudeness, and because he did not have a proper attitude to his comrades, and was capricious and abused his power.

In December 1922, in a letter to the party congress, Vladimir Ilyich wrote: 'After taking over the position of Secretary-General Comrade Stalin accumulated in his hands immense power and I am not sure whether he will always be able to use this power with the required care'. This letter,—a political document of tremendous importance, known in the party history as Lenin's 'testament'—was distributed among the delegates to the Twentieth Party Congress. You have read it, and will undoubtedly read it again more than once. You might reflect on Lenin's plain words: 'Stalin is excessively rude, and this defect which can be freely tolerated in our midst and in contacts among us Communists becomes a defect which cannot be tolerated in someone holding the position of Secretary-General. Because of this I propose that the comrades consider how to remove Stalin from this position and select someone else for it, someone who would above all differ from Stalin in one single quality, namely, greater tolerance, greater loyalty, greater kindness and a more considerate attitude towards his comrades, and a less capricious temper . . .'

This document of Lenin's was made known to the delegates to the Thirteenth Party Congress, who discussed the question of transferring Stalin. The delegates declared themselves in favour of retaining Stalin in his post, hoping that he would heed Vladimir Ilyich's critical remarks and would be able to overcome the defects which caused Lenin such serious anxiety...

When we analyse Stalin's practice in regard to the direction of the party and the country, when we pause to consider everything which Stalin perpetrated, we must be convinced that Lenin's fears were justified. Stalin's negative characteristics which in Lenin's time were only incipient transformed themselves later into a grave abuse of power which caused untold harm to the party.

We have to consider this matter seriously and analyse it correctly in order to preclude any possibility of a repetition in any form whatever of what took place during Stalin's life. He did not tolerate collective leadership or work and practised brutal violence not only towards everything which opposed him but also towards anything which his capricious and despotic character found to be against his concepts.

Stalin acted not through persuasion, explanation, and patient co-operation with people but by imposing his views and demanding absolute submission. Whoever opposed this concept or tried to prove his own viewpoint and the correctness of his position, was doomed to be removed from the leading collective and to suffer subsequent moral and physical annihilation. This was especially true during the period following the Seventeenth Party Congress when many prominent party leaders and rank-and-file workers, honest and dedicated to the cause of Communism, fell victim to Stalin's despotism.

We must say that the party had fought a serious fight against the Trotskyists, rightists, and bourgeois nationalists, and that it ideologically disarmed all the enemies of Leninism. This ideological fight was carried on successfully as a result of which the party was strengthened and tempered. Here Stalin played a positive role . . .

It is worth noting that even during the furious ideological struggle against the Trotskyists, Zinovievists, the Bukharinists and others, extreme repressive measures were not used. The fight was on ideological grounds. But some years later when Socialism in our country was fundamentally built, when the exploiting classes were generally liquidated, when the Soviet social structure had radically changed, when the social base for political movements and groups hostile to the party had violently contracted, when the ideological opponents of the party were long since defeated politically—then the repression against them began.

It was precisely during this period (1935—1937—1938) that the practice of mass repression through the Government apparatus was born, first against the enemies of Leninism— Trotskyists, Zinovievists, Bukharinists, who had been long since defeated by the party—and subsequently also against many honest Communists, against those party cadres who had borne the heavy load of the Civil War and the first and most difficult years of industrialisation and collectivisation, who actively fought against the Trotskyists and the rightists for the Leninist party line.

Stalin originated the concept 'enemy of the people'. This term automatically rendered it unnecessary that the ideological errors of a man or men engaged in a controversy be proved; this term made possible the usage of the most cruel repression, violating all norms of revolutionary legality, against anyone who in any way disagreed with Stalin, against those who were only suspected of hostile intent, or against those who had bad reputations. This concept 'enemy of the people' actually eliminated the possibility of any kind of ideological struggle or the making of one's views known on this or that issue, even those of a practical nature. In the main and in fact, the only proof of guilt used, against all norms of current science, was the 'confession' of the accused himself; and as subsequent investigation proved, 'confessions' were obtained through physical duress against the accused.

D

This led to glaring violations of revolutionary legality, and to the fact that many entirely innocent people who in the past had defended the party line became victims . . . It is a fact that many persons who were later annihilated as 'enemies of the people' had worked with Lenin during his life. Some of these persons had made errors during Lenin's life but in spite of this Lenin benefited from their work, he corrected them, and did everything possible to retain them in the ranks of the party; he induced them to follow him . . .

Stalin discarded Lenin's method of convincing and educating; he abandoned the method of ideological struggle for that of administrative violence, mass repression, and terror. He acted on an increasingly large scale and more stubbornly through punitive organs, often violating all existing norms of morality and Soviet law.

Arbitrary behaviour by one man encouraged and permitted arbitrariness in others. Mass arrests and deportations of many thousands of people, execution without trial and without the normal investigation created conditions of insecurity, fear, and desperation . . .

It has been determined that of the 139 members and candidates of the central committee who were elected at the Seventeenth Congress in 1934, 98 people i.e. 70 per cent were arrested and shot (mostly in 1937–8). (Indignation in the hall.)

What was the composition of the delegates to the Seventeenth Congress? It is known that 80 per cent of the voting participants joined the party during the years of conspiracy before the Revolution and during the Civil War; this means before 1921. By social origin the basic mass of the delegates were workers (60 per cent of the voting members).

For this reason it was inconceivable that a congress so composed would have elected a central committee, a majority of whom would prove to be enemies of the party . . .

The same fate befell not only the central committee members but also the majority of the delegates to the congress. Of 1,966 delegates with either voting or advisory rights, 1,108 persons were arrested on charges of counter-revolutionary crimes, i.e. decidedly more than a majority. This very fact shows how absurd, wild and contrary to common sense were the charges of counter-revolutionary crimes made out, as we now see, against a majority of participants at the Seventeenth Party Congress. (Indignation in the hall) . . .

Facts prove that many abuses were made on Stalin's orders without reckoning with any norms of party and Soviet legality. Stalin was a very distrustful man, diseased with suspicion; we knew this from our work with him. He could look at a man and say: 'Why are your eyes so shifty today?' or 'Why are you turning away so much today and avoiding looking me straight in the eye?' This sickly suspicion created in him a general distrust even towards eminent party workers whom he had known for years. Everywhere and in everything he saw 'enemies', 'double-dealers', and 'spies'.

Possessing unlimited power he indulged in great wilfulness and strangled a person morally and physically. A situation was created where one could not express one's own will . . .

The policy of large-scale repression against the military cadres undermined military discipline, because for several years officers of all ranks and even soldiers in the party cells were taught to 'unmask' their superiors as hidden enemies . . . Many commanders perished in camps and gaols and the army saw them no more. All this brought about the situation which existed at the beginning of the war and which was a great threat to our fatherland.

It would be wrong to forget that after the first severe disaster and defeats at the front Stalin thought that this was the end. In one of his speeches during those days he said: 'All that Lenin created we have lost for ever'. For a long time after this Stalin actually did not direct military operations and stopped doing anything at all. He returned to active leadership only when some Politburo members visited him and told him it was necessary to take immediate steps to improve the situation at the front.

So the danger which hung over our fatherland in the first period of the war was largely due to the methods of directing the nation and party adopted by Stalin himself. However, we speak not just of the moment when the war began, which led to serious disorganisation of our army and brought us severe losses. Even after the war began, the nervousness and hysteria which Stalin showed by interfering with actual military operations caused our army serious damage.

Stalin was very far from understanding the real situation which was developing at the front. This was natural because during the whole war he never visited any section of the front or any liberated city except for one short ride on the Mozhaisk highway during a stabilised situation at the front. To this incident were dedicated numerous literary works full of all kinds of fantasies and many paintings . . .

Some comrades may ask us: 'Where were the members of the Politburo? Why didn't they assert themselves against the cult of the individual in time? And why is this only being done now?' First of all we have to consider the fact that Politburo members viewed these matters in a different way at different times. Initially, many of them backed Stalin actively because he was one of the strongest Marxists, and his logic, his will, and his strength greatly influenced the cadres and party work.

It is known that Stalin, after Lenin's death, especially during the first years actively fought for Leninism against the enemies of Leninist theory and against those who deviated. Beginning with Leninist theory the party, with the central committee at its head, started on a grand scale the work of socialist industrialisation, agricultural collectivisation, and the cultural revolution. At that time Stalin gained great popularity, sympathy, and support . . . Later, however, abusing his power more and more Stalin began to fight eminent party and Government leaders and to use terroristic methods against honest Soviet people . . . Attempts to oppose groundless suspicions and charges resulted in the opponent himself falling victim to the repression . . .

In the situation which then prevailed I often talked with Nikolai Aleksandrovich Bulganin; once when we two were travelling in a car, he said 'It has happened sometimes that a man goes to Stalin on his invitation as a friend. And when he sits with Stalin, he does not know where he will be sent next, home or to gaol'.

Obviously such conditions put every member of the Politburo in a very difficult situation. And when we also consider the fact that in the last years the central committee plenary sessions were not convened and that Politburo sessions only occurred from time to time, then we will understand how hard it was for any Politburo member to take a stand against one or other unjust or improper procedure, and against serious errors and shortcomings in the practice of leadership . . .

SOURCE: Speech of N. S. Khruschev at the Twentieth Party Congress of the Communist Party of the Soviet Union (25 February 1956); published by the United States Department of State (1956)

PART TWO

The People Take to the Streets

Khruschev's speech at the Twentieth Party Congress had an effect which the Kremlin cannot have anticipated. Its profoundest impact was outside the Soviet Union in the 'people's democracies'. The speech was the climax of an extraordinary year.

During 1955–6 people in Eastern Europe watched a threefold process develop. First there was the end of the purges, the rehabilitation of their victims, official criticism of the security police and curtailment of their powers. Then came the Soviet-Yugoslav rapprochement. Not only was national Communism being endorsed by Moscow, but the leading rebel against Stalinism was being publicly feted by the Soviet leadership. Finally Khruschev had turned the spotlight towards the heart of the system with his Congress speech. It was now possible to go behind the euphemisms about 'socialist construction' and examine the way Communist power had actually been used in the first 8 or 10 years of its existence in the 'people's democracies'.

Within the various Communist parties and among socialist intellectuals the impact was immediate. It caused a renaissance of faith in socialist ideals, and opened up at last the prospect of reform. Lifelong Socialists who had joined in the take-over of power after the war and had then seen their hopes dashed by the cruel distortions of the early 1950s felt new optimism. There was a chance for a second start. The fate of the tentative economic reform after Stalin's death, when the New Course was begun

54

and partially abandoned, might have been something of a warning against exaggerated hopes. But now in the spring of 1956 the perspectives seemed wider. The whole political system was under examination. The possibility of each country experimenting according to its own local conditions looked real.

These sudden new perspectives affected a larger circle of people than merely the reformist groups in the Communist parties or the intelligentsia. Soviet control over Eastern Europe had begun to seem looser. The pent-up nationalistic feelings that have never been far from the surface in Eastern Europe were aroused. Traditional antagonism towards the Soviet Union was strong in every country except Czechoslovakia and Bulgaria. It was now to come out again.

Yet, surprisingly perhaps, only two countries, Poland and Hungary were deeply convulsed by the movement which Khruschev had set in motion. In the other countries the conservative local Stalinist leadership kept control, using the argument of the imperialist threat to the socialist camp to ward off questions about the Stalinist system. In Bulgaria, Czechoslovakia, East Germany and Rumania conservatives squashed the reformist trend within the party long before liberalisation could spill over into the streets.

In Poland and Hungary the pressures were stronger. People raised the cry for independence and for a new political system. In Poland the movement was barely contained and diverted into reformist channels after the Soviet Union was persuaded to hold back from using force. But in Hungary it became a nationalist uprising provoked largely by the Soviet Union's own initial intervention with tanks and armoured vehicles. Once they appeared on the streets of Budapest and other cities, the situation was changed. By the time they started to withdraw a few days later after desperate appeals from the Hungarian Government the possibility of a 'Polish' solution had been overtaken.

In the meantime British and French troops had landed at Suez, allegedly to separate the advancing Israeli troops from the Egyptians. The Russians felt justifiably confident that the West was too involved in the Middle East to prevent a Russian intervention in Hungary, even though President Eisenhower and Mr Dulles were expressing deep concern in the United Nations Security Council. Some Hungarians began to call for neutrality for their country. They were egged on by broadcasts from the American radio station Radio Free Europe. The Hungarian Government followed suit and proclaimed neutrality. The whole balance of power in Europe was brought into question and the Russians returned with overwhelming force to smash the revolt.

The Soviet experiment in allowing more latitude to its East European neighbours was thus stillborn. Khruschev's reconciliation with Tito was reversed and the polemics between Moscow and Belgrade went back to their earlier vitriolic level. In the space of 2 months the perspectives opened up in the spring of 1956 were blacked out. The Dark Ages seemed to have returned.

HUNGARY 1956

The Hungarian party leadership reacted to Khruschev's secret speech like an ostrich. Its policy barely changed. Organised calls for reform were left initially to the country's intellectuals, Communists and non-Communists alike.

As in other authoritarian societies, particularly those which have known frequent invasions and occupations, intellectuals had traditionally acquired a political role. For centuries the Hungarian nation had retained its cultural identity through the voice of its writers and poets.

In 1956 they came into their own again. A club of young intellectuals known as the Petöfi Circle, after Hungary's romantic Byron-like poet of the nineteenth century, became the centre of activity. The circulations of literary periodicals rose, as writers began to articulate the suppressed grievances of many years and probe into previously unpublicised aspects of the country's life. No one document can do justice to the range of issues touched on. But this slightly coy extract from the journal Irodalmi Ujsag *(18 August 1956) entitled 'Unpleasant Questions' and by Judith Mariassy gives the flavour.*

14 Judith Mariassy
UNPLEASANT QUESTIONS

During a recent union meeting in a factory, the secretary mentioned that he had been on a vacation abroad. The group with which he had travelled, he said, was accompanied by one of the secretaries of the National Council of Trade Unions. 'Naturally' the secretary of the NCTU lived in a separate resort hotel and once in a while drove over to the workers to see how they were doing. Why does it have to be this way, he asked, and why do they have to put up a fence around the resort in Balaton-Aliga and station guards where workers of the party centre spend their holiday?

His questions received enthusiastic applause. Another worker stood up: 'I share comrade secretary's opinion. I would like to make a suggestion: separate tailor shops and department stores should not be set up for party leaders. It would be much better if party leaders received more pay, but purchased food and clothing in stores where we do our shopping and at the same price. That way they will know all the time what the standard of living is, what people need, which prices have gone up, and what help is needed'.

Not long ago I went for a walk with a foreign newspaperman on the Szabadsaghegy. We came to a large, fenced-in area somewhere around Bela Kiraly Avenue. An AVR guard stood there with a gun. 'Who lives here?', asked my foreign friend. I could not answer. 'Why don't you ask the soldier?' I remained silent. I could not say aloud what I thought: 'I have an idea he would not give a very polite reply'.

SOURCE: Reprinted from *Hungarian Social Science Reader (1945–1963)*, edited by Dr William Juhasz, Aurora Editions (Munich 1965)

In the absence of changes from within the party the Soviet leaders decided to step in to promote the necessary minimum of de-Stalinisation. In July two Politburo members, Suslov and Mikoyan, came to Budapest and asked Matyas Rakosi, the party leader, to resign.

His successor, Ernest Gerö, was hardly a reformer. The programme he proposed was full of half-measures and contradictions—a widening of Parliament's role and the rehabilitation of more political prisoners, but no end to collectivisation or to the emphasis on heavy industry.

*The party leadership under its new head still had little credit, and
for the next 3 months popular pressures for reform increased. Demands
grew for a full-scale funeral for Laszlo Rajk, the former Foreign
Minister, who had been rehabilitated posthumously a year earlier but
only in a grudging way. At the beginning of October Gerö gave in. The
funeral for him and three other executed colleagues became the occasion
for a huge and totally peaceful march through the streets of Budapest.
At its head walked Rajk's widow and Imre Nagy, who had been expelled
again from the central committee after Malenkov's fall. Antal Apro, a
member of the Politburo, spoke to the crowd after the march.*

15 Antal Apro
THE BURIAL OF LASZLO RAJK

Dear mourners, dear comrades:

We have never fulfilled a more difficult and more tragic
duty than now when we say farewell to our outstanding comrades and friends, Laszlo Rajk, Tibor Szonyi, Gyorgy Palffy,
and Andras Szalai, who were sentenced to death on the basis of
provocative false charges in 1949. We are fulfilling a comradely
duty of honor now in burying the earthly remains of our comrades beside the graves of the martyrs of the 1919 dictatorship
of the proletariat, the dead heroes of the illegal battles and of
the Hungarian Workers' movement. We are performing the
last acts of the rehabilitation demanded by the Central Committee of our Party and the will of the people.

We are aware that not even the most complete rehabilitation
can change what has already happened, that we cannot
resurrect our dear comrades no matter how we pay respects to
their memory. We can not completely heal the wound caused
by their death in the hearts of the members of their families, a
wound which, even if only temporarily, weakened faith in the
higher morality and justice of socialism in the eyes of many
hundreds of thousands of Hungarian workers. Our hearts are
filled with bitterness and sorrow as we stand in front of the
graves of our comrades who died the death of martyrs, because

we gave credit to false accusations seven years ago and could not save their lives for the good of the country and of the Party.

We deeply regret that serious mistakes and crimes led to this tragedy for our comrades. Their martyrdom also contributed to our awakening to the fact, albeit imperfectly and tardily, that serious political mistakes of far-reaching consequences had appeared in our work, in addition to the wonderful achievements of our people in the course of building socialism and the new Hungary.

In many cases, a leadership practice completely alien to socialism had gained control in the leadership of our Party and our state before 1953. Socialist legality was often violated, and so was the constitution and human freedom, and as a consequence, the cause of the building of socialism and the ideas of socialist humanism in many cases were separated from each other. This caused immeasurable harm not only in our internal political life, but also hurt seriously our People's Republic on the international scene and damaged the authority of our Party among friends and sympathizers living in other countries. We call to account those persons in the leadership of the Party and the state who committed these shameful illegal acts.

The ashes of Laszlo Rajk and his fellow martyrs also mean eternal remembrance. We shall never forget that the building of socialism must also bring the complete victory of humanism in all fields of life, at all times.

For several decades our Party marched in the vanguard of the fight for Hungarian progress and liberty, even during the most difficult years of oppression. Hungarian Communists made many sacrifices for the liberty of the people. We were the only Party after the liberation which had a clear program, which did not hesitate but organized and led the fight of the working class and of the entire working population in order to put this country, defeated and destroyed in war, back on its feet again. The Party was held in respect and esteem by the working people, because the Party never had a policy contrary to the interests of the people.

We always spoke up bravely for the international cooperation of the workers, for the cause of defending peace. It is all
the more painful that tragedies such as those claiming our
martyred comrades could happen after such significant
successes. But the Party is not afraid to tell the truth now either,
to speak openly, and point out faults and abuses.

The Party and the government seriously condemn what has
happened. Before the graves of our comrades, we vow in the
name of every Hungarian Communist that we will learn from
the mistakes of the past and do everything to assure that such
monstrous acts as those to which our dear comrades fell victims
will never again take place.

We well know that there were many among the people of
good will whose faith in the Party of socialism was shaken, and
who drew conclusions from the crimes of certain leaders of
socialist construction as to the fallibility of the idea of socialism
itself, and doubted the leading role of the Party directing the
worker-peasant state in the socialist changeover when the
Central Leadership of our Party openly revealed the grave
illegal acts and publicly uncovered the abuses.

There were people who lost their faith in the future and
doubted the correctness of the basic direction of our road toward
socialism. Our many hundreds of thousands of members, the
majority of our working class, of our people, did not falter,
however. Strong men who determined to continue masters and
builders of our socialist country, they were indeed moved and
shaken by what happened but at the same time they were also
tempered and armored by it. The decisive majority of Communist workers, peasants, and intellectuals did not simply
lament and bewail the mistakes and crimes committed, but
they looked ahead into the future, searching for an assurance
that what happened with comrade Rajk and the other martyred
comrades would never again happen.

For many people the question arises: 'What assurance is there
that similar illegalities and abuses will not occur in the future?'
This is a valid question. We are obliged to answer this question

here in front of our people. The assurance is the Party. We Communists are the assurance, the many hundreds of thousands of members of our Party, because we possess the ability and the firm resolution that we will learn from the mistakes of the past. If after 1953 there was indeed still some hesitation, and there was, we firmly liquidated and shall continue to liquidate all vacillation. This is proved by the July resolution of the Central Leadership as well as its execution.

Our Party has the ability and the will to talk openly of its mistakes and at the same time to point ahead and keep directing and organizing the fight for new victories. This endeavor of ours is helped and supported by all workers who love their country.

A further assurance is the Hungarian working people, whose increased participation in the conduct of the affairs of the state, in the economy, and in society is crucially important and necessary in the interest of our further development. A further assurance is the broad development of socialist democracy in our public life and the vigorous continuation of the building of socialism. We must assure the initiative and control of the masses of the people in all fields of our social life. At the same time we are increasing our vigilance not only over the subversive activity of the enemies of our people's democratic order who still exist, but also over those who are attempting to hinder the Party's brave determination to draw the proper conclusions from the mistakes committed, as well as over those who use these mistakes as excuses for breaking through the frame of socialist democracy to open a road for bourgeois democracy and with it the reconstruction of capitalism.

Let us make a vow before the graves of Laszlo Rajk and the other comrades that we shall do everything to create guarantees that similar illegalities will never again occur, so that the cause of the Party and of the people, of the working class and of the nation of socialist construction and of humanism, may never be separated from each other . . .

Source: *Magyar Nemzet* (7 October 1956), English translation in *Hungarian Social Science Reader* (*1945–1963*), edited by Dr William Juhasz, Aurora Editions (Munich 1965)

The funeral march for Laszlo Rajk showed the depth and sincerity of the reform movement. Again the party leadership failed to understand it. Nothing was done. Two months later on 22 October the writers in the Petöfi Circle formulated a list of demands. They were moderate in tone and socialist in content.

16 Petöfi Circle
THE WRITERS' DEMANDS

1. We demand an independent national policy inspired by the principles of socialism. Our relations with other countries, including Soviet Russia and the people's democracies, must be based on the principle of equality. We demand the revision of all previously concluded economic agreements, in a spirit of equality of rights of the nations concerned.

2. We demand the end of the policies now in effect in relation to national minorities . . .

3. We demand that the Government frankly disclose the economic situation of the country . . .

4. The factories must be managed by the workers and specialists. The wage system must be reformed . . . The trade-unions must above all represent the interests of the working class.

5. Agricultural policies must be revised, and the peasants must be granted the right to determine their fate.

6. The Rakosi clique must be eliminated from public life. Imre Nagy, this noble and courageous Communist who enjoys the people's confidence, and who in the course of the last few years has consistently fought for Socialist democracy, must be appointed to the high post he deserves. At the same time we must take the necessary measures to frustrate all counter-revolutionary plans.

7. The situation requires that the Patriotic Popular Front represent the labouring classes of Hungary. Our electoral system must be brought into conformity with the requirements of a Socialist democracy. The people's representatives in Parliament and in all autonomous branches of the administration must be elected by secret ballot.

SOURCE: *Behind the Rape of Hungary*, by François Fejtö (New York 1957)

On the same day as the writers, the students drew up their demands. As might be expected, they were more far-reaching.

17 THE STUDENTS' DEMANDS

1. We demand the immediate evacuation of all Soviet troops, in conformity with the provisions of the peace treaty.

2. We demand the election by secret ballot of all party members from top to bottom, and of new officers for the lower, middle, and upper echelons of the Hungarian Workers' Party. These officers shall convoke a party congress as early as possible in order to elect a central committee.

3. A new Government must be constituted under the direction of Comrade Imre Nagy; all the criminal leaders of the Stalin-Rakosi era must be immediately relieved of their duties.

4. We demand a public enquiry into the criminal activities of Mihaly Farkas [the police chief] and his accomplices. Matyas Rakosi, who is the person most responsible for all the crimes in the recent past, as well as for the ruin of our country, must be brought back to Hungary for trial before a people's tribunal.

5. We demand that general elections, by universal secret ballot, be held throughout the country to elect a new National Assembly, with all political parties participating. We demand that the right of workers to strike be recognised.

6. We demand revision and re-adjustment of Hungarian-Soviet and Hungarian-Yugoslav relations in the fields of politics, economics, and cultural affairs, on a basis of complete political and economic equality and of non-interference in the internal affairs of one by the other.

7. We demand the complete re-organisation of Hungary's economic life under the direction of specialists. The entire economic system, based on a system of planning, must be re-examined in the light of conditions in Hungary and in the vital interests of the Hungarian people.

8. Our foreign trade agreements and the exact total of reparations that can never be paid must be made public. We demand precise and exact information on the uranium deposits in our country, on their exploitation, and on the concessions accorded the Russians in this area. We demand that Hungary have the right to sell her uranium freely at world market prices to obtain hard currency.

9. We demand complete revision of the norms in effect in industry and an immediate and radical adjustment of salaries in accordance with the just requirements of workers and intellectuals. We demand that a minimum living wage be fixed for workers.

10. We demand that the system of distribution be organised on a new basis and that agricultural products be utilised in a rational manner. We demand equality of treatment for individual farms.

11. We demand reviews by independent tribunals of all political and economic trials as well as the release and rehabilitation of the innocent. We demand the immediate repatriation of prisoners of war and of civilian deportees in the Soviet Union, including prisoners sentenced outside Hungary.

12. We demand complete recognition of freedom of opinion and of expression, of freedom of the press and of radio, as well as the creation of a new daily newspaper for the MEFESZ organisation (Hungarian Federation of University and College Students' Associations).

13. We demand that the statue of Stalin, symbol of Stalinist tyranny and political oppression, be removed as quickly as possible and be replaced by a monument to the memory of the martyred fighters for freedom of 1848–1849.

14. We demand the replacement of the emblems that are foreign to the Hungarian people by the old Hungarian arms of Kossuth. We demand for the Hungarian army new uniforms conforming to our national traditions. We demand that the fifteenth of March be declared a national holiday and that the sixth of October be a day of national mourning, on which schools will be closed.

15. The students of the Technical University of Budapest declare unanimously their solidarity with the workers and students of Warsaw and Poland in their movement toward national independence.

16. The students of the Technical University of Budapest will organise as rapidly as possible local branches of the MEFESZ, and they have decided to convoke at Budapest, on Saturday, October 27, a Youth Parliament at which all the nation's youth will be represented by their delegates.

SOURCE: *Nepszava* (23 October 1956); reprinted in *Thirteen Days that Shook the Kremlin*, by Tibor Meray. © 1959 by Frederick A. Praeger, Inc, New York. Excerpted and printed by permission

After preparing their demands the students called a mass rally for 23 October. Its purpose was to express solidarity with Poland, where after some days of uncertainty the Russians had just decided not to intervene by force to prevent the election of a new party leadership under Wladyslaw Gomulka.

Thousands of people converged on 23 October on the statue of Jozsef Bem, the Polish general who had helped the Hungarians in the revolution of 1848. Writers and students read out their demands. The crowds did not disperse. The streets were full of expectant people. Some shots were fired near the radio building. During the evening an

E

emergency central committee meeting was held, and Nagy was called back as Prime Minister.

Gerö stayed on as first secretary of the party. At the same time a secret message was sent, probably by him, to the Soviet leadership asking for the Soviet garrison in Hungary to intervene to help to restore order.

The sudden arrival of Russian tanks inevitably inflamed the crowds. Street fighting developed. Over the next few days there was total confusion with sporadic clashes between people and the tanks and a vacuum of effective leadership in Budapest. In several parts of the country revolutionary committees were set up. Numerous factories were taken over by workers' councils, whose formation was encouraged by the trade union leadership, and sanctioned, probably despairingly, by the central committee of the party.

18 Radio Kossuth
THE ELECTION OF WORKERS' COUNCILS

The central committee approves the election of workers' councils through the intermediary of the trade union organs.

It is known that the presidium of the SZOT (National Council of Trade Unions) passed a resolution on this matter. The presidium of SZOT recommends that workers and employees establish worker management in the factories, plants, mines, and everywhere else and elect workers' councils.

1. As for the operation of the workers' councils, we suggest that the members of the councils be elected by all the workers of the factory, plant, or mine. The form of election should be decided by a meeting called together for the purpose of elections. Nominations for the council should be made generally by the factory committee or a respected worker. The council should have 21–27 members depending on the size of the factory and every group of workers should be represented in proportion to their number. In factories employing less than a hundred workers the council may consist of all the workers.

2. The tasks of the workers' council: the council decides all problems in connexion with production and management in

the factory. First: for the direction of management and production they should elect from their number a council consisting of ten to fifteen members to aid the permanent manager, which will decide problems concerning the management of the factory, following the direct orders of the workers' council. It may hire or dismiss workers and the technical and economic directors of the factory. Second: it will work out the production plan of the plant and set up the system of norms in mechanical production. Third: the workers' council determines the most suitable pay system for the particular plant and the development of the social and cultural provisions of the plant. Fourth: it determines questions of investment and the use of the profit share. Fifth: it is to lay down the plan of work of the factory, mine, or plant. Sixth: it is responsible to all the workers and the state for proper management.

The present task of the workers' councils is to assure order, discipline, and start production.

All workers, supported by the entire electorate are to protect their source of bread—the factory.

SOURCE: Broadcast by Radio Kossuth (26 October 1956) as a communiqué from the Hungarian Workers' Party; reprinted from the English translation in Juhasz, op cit

Nagy was torn between the desires of the Russians, who had temporarily pacified the capital and were able to see that some reforms were essential, and the unceasing demands pouring in from the numerous local committees. Nagy approached the leaders of the former Social Democratic and Peasant parties. He felt the socialist economy could be maintained within the framework of a multi-party coalition. The Russians had begun uneasily to withdraw their troops from Budapest.

But voices were now raised calling for the country's complete independence and Hungary's departure from the Warsaw Pact. After days of agonising Nagy gave in to this demand. Neutrality was proclaimed.

The Soviet leaders decided they had to intervene again. On 4 November the tanks entered Budapest for the second time and ended the revolt.

The Hungarian army remained largely passive. Two or three of the biggest factories held out for several days. Hundreds of people died in street fighting.

A 'revolutionary workers' and peasants' Government' was installed under Janos Kadar, who had replaced Gerö as first secretary after the first Soviet intervention. For a few weeks there was a political stalemate in spite of the Soviet military superiority. A central workers' council for Budapest acted as an unofficial opposition. The Government had little support. It invited Nagy, who had taken refuge in the Yugoslav embassy, to come out on a promise that there would be no reprisals.

In December the mood changed. Nagy was deported to the Soviet Union (and executed 2 years later). The political police were restored. The leaders of the central workers' council were arrested.

It was no surprise that Yugoslavia reacted sharply to the Hungarian crisis. The Soviet-Yugoslav rapprochement was in jeopardy again. Yet the exact nature of the second stage of the Hungarian uprising puzzled even President Tito. Was it revolution or counter-revolution? Was it socialist or anti-socialist?

In a speech at Pula soon after the events Tito was equivocal about it, although he criticised the first intervention. On 6 December his vice-president and chief theoretician Edward Kardelj elaborated the Yugoslav position more fully in a speech to the Federal Assembly in Belgrade.

Kardelj's analysis was an attempt to interpret the Hungarian events in Marxist terms. It spelled out the clear ideological differences between the Soviet Union and the Yugoslav vision of socialism with its emphasis on workers' councils and the development of democracy at the base of society in order to counteract bureaucratic tendencies at the top.

In the first flush of the 1948 dispute, when the Yugoslavs broke with Moscow, there had been no such well defined ideological statement of the differences. Eight years later the dust had settled. The Yugoslavs were able to work out their own theory of how socialism must develop if it was to survive. This gave Kardelj's speech a particular importance.

19 Edward Kardelj
SOCIALISM MUST DEVELOP

. . . The latest events in Hungary are a further warning to those who are not prepared to accept facts as facts, and who believe that with the victory of the revolution and the assumption of power by a Communist party, objective social laws cease to be applicable. On the contrary they will avenge themselves on anyone who tries to ignore them.

The actual leading social role of the Communist party cannot be decreed by law. The party can indeed be a leading one; that is, it can be the most progressive social factor, but only in cases where it really works according to objective social laws. Since these laws act through men, through social classes, the Communist party or any other leading organised socialist force in the transitional period from capitalism to socialism must be in such a position that the most progressive socialist tendencies can be expressed through it, as well as through the entire social mechanism, and that it itself changes with the development of socialist relations.

If a party does not understand this, then I do not know how it can beat its Communist chest and boast of Marxism-Leninism, referring to its leading historical role. On the contrary it will play the role of a brake on socialist development.

It can even become a reactionary force if it doggedly continues in this direction. The belief that a party, by the very fact that it calls itself Communist, assures a progressive and democratic character to its rule is a grave, anti-Marxist blunder. This has been clearly shown in Hungary. There, an anti-democratic system of bureaucratic despotism for years pursued the determined and wilful policy of a clique against the will of the working masses. This eventually brought about an armed action in which the main force was the working class, that is, precisely that class which alone can be the agent of socialist transformation in Hungarian society . . .

Socialism in the final stage must be liberated from bureaucratic brakes and be able to develop by its internal experience, strengthen itself and grow by the stability and internal force of the social initiative of the broad masses organised on the basis of social ownership of the means of production.

Precisely for this reason there can be no progress of socialism without a parallel development of specific forms of democracy which correspond to the socialist economic base. In our country this principle was applied in practice sometimes with more and sometimes with less success, but it was applied on an increasingly wide front . . .

On the basis of this, a few essentially practical questions have to be put to impartial Marxist analysis. First of all, if it is a question of specific mistakes of the Rakosi-Gerö clique alone, and not the bureaucratic system which began to play a reactionary role with regard to socialist development, why then did the Hungarian working masses have to resort to the use of force and arms to stand up against the policy responsible for these mistakes? . . . What consolation is it to the socialist conscience to contend that the working class, eleven years after its own victory, was taken in by the counter-revolution? Even if this were true, the question must be asked: should the stick be broken on the head of the working class or the political system which put the working class in the absurd position of allegedly fighting its own historic interests?

Such logic can only lead to the absurd conclusion which has no connection with socialism let alone with Marxism, that a party or state can build socialism without the working class or even against its will. In fact, the Hungarian working class has spontaneously acted in a socialist way and only in a socialist way. However, it has with regard to conceptions of the state system, democracy, and political and party relations, been very much under the influence of various petty bourgeois abstract imperialist ideas, yet at the same time, it has stood firmly for its ownership of the means of production.

What is more, it further developed its successes by setting up workers' councils, transforming the means of production from state property to consistent social ownership, that is, ownership under direct democratic management of the community of producers. It is also characteristic that workers declared themselves for united workers' councils and for the higher association of the councils, so that they would exercise a direct influence on the central state authority. This in itself shows that the Hungarian working class, despite the ideological confusion into which it was led, nevertheless spontaneously found the essentially right way to power.

Of course it is difficult to say whether in the further course of the struggle for power the Hungarian working class could succeed in holding these positions in factories. There is no doubt that the vampire-like, bourgeois-reactionary forces, which would have undoubtedly received increasing support from abroad, might have tried to bring their victory to a conclusion . . .

It would be a great mistake and illusion to believe that in the final form of Nagy's Government as it existed before 4 November, the revolutionary clashes in Hungary took their normal course. On the contrary the battle for the final social and political form in Hungary had then only begun, and no honest person could guess where it would end.

It was of course probable that socialist forces would have succeeded in preserving the socialist economic basis of Hungarian society. In any case, the working class would have had to shed much more blood and live through many more disappointments before it could, through struggle and defeat, gain the experience which would enable it empirically to create a new democratic mechanism of the socialist social system.

However a serious defeat of the working class and socialism could not be excluded. Thus Hungary could have become the cause of a very dangerous international clash. It was in this light that we viewed the second Soviet intervention in Hungary. We are of course in principle against any foreign intervention regardless of its source, not only because of the right of nations to settle their internal differences themselves, but also because intervention, when it is a matter of a social crisis, never solves problems. It can only postpone settlement for a limited time and simultaneously intensify problems . . .

However we also believed it possible that Soviet intervention in the situation peculiar to Hungary would be the lesser evil, that is, if it could reduce the likelihood of further bloodshed and allow a Government and a policy to be set up in Hungary which would, on the basis of a changed political system, gather together all socialist forces and insure the working class through workers' councils and other similar working class organs influence in state politics which it lacked in the past. Only such positive consequences could have justified Soviet intervention. If these results do not appear, the very act of intervention will be historically condemned . . .

SOURCE: *The Soviet-Yugoslav Controversy*, op cit

POLAND 1956

The first signs of major changes in Poland came a few weeks after Khruschev's dramatic speech. Wladyslaw Gomulka, the former party secretary, was released, together with eight co-accused. A month later under a general amnesty some 30,000 political prisoners were freed. The party leader, Edward Ochab, promised to revitalise the Parliament.

In June, however, an explosive event occurred. A delegation of workers and party members from a huge locomotive and armaments factory in Poznan went to Warsaw to see trade union and Government officials with a string of complaints about low wages and bad conditions. They were rebuffed. A peaceful march by the workers left behind in Poznan suddenly took on a nationalist turn with slogans such as 'Down with the USSR' and 'Down with Soviet occupation' alongside the placards with their specific complaints. Polish army tanks were sent in, and after several hours of violence 54 people lay dead.

Subsequently the Polish leadership realised that the workers' grievances about wages were justified, and that Poznan was only a symbol of countrywide dissatisfaction. They decided to continue with the reform instead of halting it. Gomulka was reinstated into the party. The

Politburo was enlarged, and the central committee outlined a programme to raise living standards and give workers a role in running factories.

Throughout the summer Poland's writers and intellectuals had begun pushing the limits of censorship wider. Within the party voices calling for a radical change were becoming bolder. One of the most influential of these was a young philosopher, Leszek Kolakowski, who had taught for a time at the party college.

In September Nowe Drogi, *the theoretical monthly of the central committee, published his article 'Intellectuals and the Communist Movement' from which these excerpts are taken. It had a profound effect in party ranks.*

20 Leszek Kolakowski
MARX NEEDS TO BE RESURRECTED

In the present condition of Marxist theory one might well wish Karl Marx could be resurrected. But since that is highly unlikely, the theoretical work that is supposed to create for the communist movement a scientific basis for political activity adequate to the needs of our times can be only a collective effort on the part of communist intellectuals, trained in various fields of knowledge about society, capable of utilising the everyday experiences of the masses, and attuned to the voice of public opinion. This is also necessary if the communist world outlook is to be able to react to the ideological life which was pulsing beneath the slogans on our banners, just as large-scale commercial activity was going on outside of state banks and official statistics.

Communist intellectuals have the responsibility to fight for the secularisation of thinking, to combat pseudo-Marxist mythology and bigotry as well as religio-magic practices, and to struggle to rebuild respect for completely unrestricted secular reason. Daily experience teaches us that this process is not ended and cannot run its course without great opposition from a large number of people (and also organisations and institutions) whose social position is supported solely by an anti-democratic method of wielding power and by a closely related anti-intellectualism. Since, as we have said, overcoming the tendency to make a fetish of the theory is in itself a condition for effective political activity on the part of the communist movement, the participation of intellectuals opposed to all mythology constitutes an indispensable prerequisite to all efforts aimed at a political rebirth of the party. The creative circles of the intelligentsia, because of their professions, are particularly sensitive to impulses of modernity in the most varied realms of life, and can most easily rid themselves of conservatism.

In order for the intelligentsia, and especially scientific circles, to fulfil their normal function, as defined by the social division of labour, we must remove the limitations that have arisen in this period as a result of the misconception of the relationship between science and politics and the wrong methods used to resolve the conflicts between them.

First of all, any political restriction on the subject matter of scientific research is damaging. Yet it continues to exist. Consequently, when one realises that the results of one's analysis in a given field can be neither published nor used, it is hard to make this field the subject of a collective research project. (This applies particularly to certain segments of political history and to the history of ideology, as well as to certain questions regarding contemporary life in the countries that have been emancipated from capitalism).

Second, it is equally harmful, in a field that is subject to scientific research, to announce that certain truths are 'politically correct' and to demand that they be disseminated without regard to scientific discussion. Whenever this is the practice, humanistic sciences are moribund and their work amounts to no more than placing garlands on the plaster of Paris façades of socialist life—which is done sincerely by those who are less discerning, and cynically by the more intelligent. Scientific cynicism is the natural product of the rape of the principles of scientific thought.

. . . The Communist party needs intellectuals not so that they can marvel at the wisdom of its decisions, but only so that its decisions will be wise. Intellectuals are necessary to communism as people who are free in their thinking, and superfluous as opportunists. Theoretical work cannot be useful to the revolutionary movement if it is controlled by anything besides scientific stringency and the striving for true knowledge; it must therefore be free for the good of the movement. That is why communist intellectuals who come to the defence of thought independent of political pressure do so not only in the name of an abstract freedom of knowledge, but also in the interests of communism, which as we have shown ever since the Communist Manifesto, has no interests—in regard to either production or culture—that are distinct from the interests of all humanity.

To make a fetish of Marxism, to reduce it to a conventional apologetic ornamentation that finds its place only on the façade of society, means that instead of being the lifeblood of intellectual life Marxism can become its poison. One should not for this reason belittle its creative capabilities. After all, even a precision instrument can be used to crush skulls. What we need for the development of Marxism is not 'new formulations' that have to be learned by rote, but an objective and highly technical analysis of new, as well as old, social phenomena . . .

SOURCE: *Marxism and Beyond*, by Leszek Kolakowski, translated by Jane Zielenko Peel (Paladin, 1971)

By mid-October pressure had mounted for a complete break with the past. As a symbol for this, liberals were calling for the appointment of Gomulka as first secretary of the party. He was considered the only man with an image sufficiently independent of Moscow to reflect the widespread desire within the party and outside it for a new, national dimension to socialism in Poland. It was a standing insult, for example, that the head of the country's armed forces and a member of the Politburo was a Soviet Marshal, Konstantin Rokossovsky.

The trend of the Polish movement had begun to worry Moscow, and the Stalinists left in the Polish leadership hoped to feed on this to prevent Gomulka's election. Anxiously during the autumn the liberals warned people to avoid demonstrations in the streets for fear of creating a 'provocation' which might bring the Russians in.

On the morning of 19 October Khruschev, with three of the Soviet Politburo members and the Commander-in-Chief of the Warsaw Pact forces, flew to Poland. Thousands of workers had sent Gomulka and the liberals letters and messages of support. The Polish secret police and the frontier guards were loyal to them. The Polish delegation, which included Gomulka, met the Soviet leaders armed with this backing and were able to argue that the reform movement was not a step back towards bourgeois democracy.

The Russians finally accepted this and flew home on 20 October. Troop movements around Poland's frontiers were cancelled, and on the same day Gomulka addressed the central committee with a fierce indictment of Stalinism and a justification of different roads to socialism. At the end of the meeting he was elected first secretary of the party.

21 Wladyslaw Gomulka
THE POLISH MODEL OF SOCIALISM

When I addressed the November Plenum of the Central Committee of the Polish United Workers' Party seven years ago, I thought that it was my last speech to the members of the Central Committee. Although only seven years have elapsed since that time or eight years since the August Plenum, where an abrupt change occurred in the party's policy, these years constitute a closed historic period. I am deeply convinced that that period has gone into the irrevocable past. There has been much evil in those years. The legacy that that period left the party, the working class, and the nation is more than alarming in certain spheres of life . . .

The working class recently gave a painful lesson to the party leadership and the Government. When seizing the weapon of strike and going out to demonstrate in the streets on that black Thursday last June, the Poznan workers shouted in a powerful voice: Enough! This cannot go on any longer! Turn back from the false road . . .

The Poznan workers did not protest against People's Poland, against socialism when they went out into the streets of the city. They protested against the evil which was widespread in our social system and which was painfully felt also by them, against the distortions of the fundamental principles of socialism, which is their idea . . .

The clumsy attempt to present the painful Poznan tragedy as the work of imperialist agents and provocateurs was very naive politically. Agents and provocateurs can and do act anywhere, but never and nowhere can they determine the attitude of the working class . . .

Among the charges which were raised against me in the past was that my attitude in different matters stemmed from an alleged lack of faith in the working class. This is not true. I have never lost faith in the wisdom, common sense, selflessness, and revolutionary attitude of the working class. In these values of the working class I believe also today. I am convinced that the Poznan workers would not have gone on strike, that they would not have demonstrated in the streets, that no men would have been found among them who even resorted to arms, that our fraternal, workers' blood would not have been shed there had the party, that is the leadership of the party, presented the whole truth to them. It was necessary to recognize without any delays the just claims of the workers; it was necessary to say what can be done today and what cannot be done; it was necessary to tell them the truth about the past and the present. There is no escaping from truth. If you cover it up, it will rise as an awful spectre, frightening, alarming, and raging madly . . .

The loss of the credit of confidence of the working class means the loss of the moral basis of power.

It is possible to govern the country even in such conditions. But then this will be bad government, for it must be based on bureaucracy, on infringing the rule of law, on violence. The essence of the dictatorship of the proletariat, as the broadest democracy for the working class and the working masses, becomes in such conditions deprived of its meaning . . . We must tell the working class the painful truth. We cannot afford at the present moment any considerable increase of wages, for the string has already been stretched so tight that it may break . . .

The road to setting up a vast network of cooperative farms in Poland's countryside is a long one. A quantitative development of producer cooperation cannot be planned because, on the basis of voluntary entry into a cooperative, this would amount to planning the growth in human consciousness, and that cannot be planned. The consciousness of the masses is shaped by their experience in life. It is shaped by facts. There are not a few facts in our present state of cooperative farming which repel the peasant masses from the cooperative farms. Such facts must be liquidated . . .

What is immutable in socialism can be reduced to the abolition of the exploitation of man by man. The roads of achieving this goal can be and are different. They are determined by various circumstances of time and place. The model of socialism can also vary. It can be such as that created in the Soviet Union; it can be shaped in a manner as we see it in Yugoslavia; it can be different still.

Only by way of the experience and achievements of various countries building socialism can the best model of socialism under given conditions arise . . .

. . . The mapping out of the Russian road to socialism passed gradually from the hands of the Central Committee into the hands of an ever smaller group of people, and finally became the monopoly of Stalin. This monopoly also encompassed the theory of scientific socialism.

The cult of personality is a specific system of exercising power, a specific road of advancing in the direction of socialism, while applying methods contrary to socialist humanism, to the socialist conception of the freedom of man, to the socialist conception of legality . . .

The cult of personality cannot be confined solely to the person of Stalin. The cult of personality is a certain system which prevailed in the Soviet Union and which was grafted on to probably all Communist Parties, as well as to a number of countries of the socialist camp, including Poland . . .

. . . In Poland, too, tragic events occurred when innocent people were sent to their death. Many others were imprisoned, often for many years, although innocent, including Communists. Many people were submitted to bestial tortures. Terror and demoralisation were spread. On the soil of the cult of personality, phenomena arose which violated and even nullified the most profound meaning of the people's power.

We have put an end to this system, or we are putting an end to it once and for all. Great appreciation should be expressed to the 20th Congress of the CPSU which so greatly helped us in the liquidation of this system . . .

The road of democratisation is the only road leading to the construction of the best model of socialism in our conditions. We shall not deviate from this road and we shall defend ourselves with all our might not to be pushed off this road. And we shall not allow anyone to use the process of democratisation to undermine socialism. Our party is taking its place at the head of the process of democratisation and only the party, acting in conjunction with the other parties of the National Front, can guide this process in a way that will truly lead to the democratisation of relations in all the spheres of our life, to the strengthening of the foundations of our system, and not to their weakening.

The party and all the people who saw the evil that existed in the past and who sincerely desire to remove all that is left of the past evil in our life today in order to strengthen the foundations of our system should give a determined rebuff to all persuasions and all voices which strive to weaken our friendship with the Soviet Union.

If in the past not everything in the relations between our party and the CPSU and between Poland and the Soviet Union shaped up in the manner it should have in our view, then today this belongs to the irrevocable past . . .

Among the many ailments of the past period was also the fact that the Sejm (Parliament) did not fulfill its constitutional task in state life. We are now facing elections to the new Sejm which ought to occupy in our political and state life the place assigned to it by the Constitution. The elevation of the role of the Sejm to that of the supreme organ of state power will probably be of the greatest importance in our democratisation program . . .

Postulating the principle of the freedom of criticism in all its forms, including criticism in the press, we have the right to demand that each criticism should be creative and just, that it should help to overcome the difficulties of the present period instead of increasing them or sometimes even treating demagogically certain phenomena and problems.

We have the right to demand from our youth, especially from university students, that they should keep their ardor in the search for roads leading to the improvement of our present reality, within the framework of the decisions which will be adopted by the present Plenum . . .

Our party should say clearly to young people: 'March in the vanguard of this great and momentous process of democratisation but always look up to your leadership, the leadership of all People's Poland, to the party of the working class, to the Polish United Workers' Party . . .

SOURCE: *National Communism and Popular Revolt in Eastern Europe*, edited by Paul Zinner (Columbia University Press, New York 1956)

The hopes roused by the Polish October were high. In contrast to what had happened in Hungary, the Polish reformers appeared to have Moscow's acquiescence. And yet the Hungarian events played a crucial role. The Polish leadership saw what had happened and grew cautious. They were afraid of the explosive popular power beneath them, and tried to act simultaneously as both reformers and gendarmes.

The vested interests of numerous middle- and lower-level party officials accumulated over a long period of bureaucratic practice could not be broken down in a hurry. In the end they overcame the reform. The workers' councils through which factory employees had powers to elect managers were converted in 1958 into 'workers' self-government conferences', which in spite of their name brought a loss of power. The press and literature turned out to be censored no longer directly by the state but by cautious, if not downright conservative, editors appointed by the party.

Stefan Kisielewski, a commentator in the liberal Catholic weekly Tygodnik Powszechny, captured the mood of immobility in an article published on 10 March 1957 under the title 'The Great Hangover or the General Impotence'.

22 Stefan Kisielewski
THE GREAT HANGOVER
OR THE GENERAL IMPOTENCE

Certain creators of October are hung over; enthusiastic youth is hung over; workers who believed in the immediate salutary effects of workers' councils are hung over; private artisans who have been allowed after many years to enter a highly difficult market deprived of raw materials are hung over; and equally hung over are the peasants who hastened to effect a devastating liquidation of the collective farms.

Even the editor-in-chief of 'Tygodnik Powszechny' is hung over: for years he dreamed of reviving his paper and today, when this has finally come about, he has found that it is very difficult and complicated and a different matter altogether from what he had expected. But particularly hung over are Marxists, of all shapes and sizes.

This latter fact worries me particularly. In the era of the Great Hangover and General Impotence, the greatest, potentially most dangerous enemy is a product of disenchantment, capable of consuming everything, namely cynicism. Cynicism stalks us, crouches, gets ready to leap and 'seek whom it may

F

devour'. The only combatants capable of fighting cynicism
are idealists; in this particular case Catholics, and Marxists.
Catholics, having gone through quite a fast in the recent period,
have saved up their enthusiasm. The Marxists are in a worse
state—they are totally hung over . . .

One can come across the results of the Marxist hangover in
some recent articles in periodicals. When I was reading them,
I had to pinch myself in the arm all the time, asking whether I
was dreaming. Are these the people who twisted our minds
in the past, and have they now been given Warsaw periodicals
for their use today? Have other, new Marxists not been found?

I believe that Marxism is on the one hand a philosophy and
on the other a socio-economic theory. But these articles are
neither philosophy nor economics; they are theology, scholast-
icism, sophistry, metaphyics, sectarianism, splitting hairs,
juggling with terms which signify nothing and interest no-one
in the present era when you can hear the pounding wings of
history. Gentlemen, redouble your efforts or make way for
others, younger than yourselves. Otherwise our joint struggle
against hangover, against apparent impotence and real
cynicism, may indeed fail . . .

*A little more than a year later Kisielewski's eager though slightly
wistful yearning for change had become embittered. By now the old
restrictions had returned to public life, as he describes in an article in
Tygodnik Powszechny of 6 July 1958.*

23 Stefan Kisielewski
CONVENTIONAL LANGUAGE

A special language rules our public, intellectual, press, and
organisational life: conventional language. It differs basically
from the spoken language used by people in everyday life.
Ordinary speech uses terms in their original meaning: they
mean what their semantic content means. In conventional
language, on the other hand, things are not called directly by

their names; they have their cryptonyms and figures of speech in the form of certain turns, phrases, and conventional expressions. This is a language as clear as the spoken one—provided you know it, that is.

I would even say that it is more precise and goes more deeply. All you need is a key. Whoever has the key—and it is not all that difficult to acquire—can read all the statements like a book and learn a multitude of things. Obviously not directly but through descriptions, metaphors, and symbols, reading between the lines. This reading between the lines is by no means a poorly judged, perfidious, or illegal activity.

Quite the contrary: the texts in question are constructed so as to be read between the lines. By their very principle, not the lines but the spaces between them are important. We can read them perfectly and it seems in no way abnormal to us: on the contrary, it is the most normal thing in the world. Personally, I am inclined to look down on people who do not know the secrets of conventional language and read it properly. These are intellectual and political primitives. Moreover, one cannot explain it to them, because the explaining can only be done in the very language they do not know . . .

SOURCE: *Tygodnik Powszechny*, Warsaw (1957 and 1958)

PART THREE

National Communism

The ending of the Hungarian uprising seemed to signal the collapse of 'national communism'. Apart from Tito—and his condemnation of the Soviet intervention was qualified by ambiguities (see Document 19)—no ruling Communist party criticised Moscow's action. Mao Tse-Tung backed Moscow fully. He rebuked Tito for making divisive remarks and proclaimed that the Soviet Union was still the centre of the international Communist movement.

Yet later events were to show that the apparent unity displayed in the autumn of 1956 was precarious. Ideological disputes soon broke out again within Eastern Europe and between the Soviet Union and China. The objective tendencies which lay behind these disputes were strong and irreversible.

The Soviet Union had begun to achieve a nuclear balance with the United States. This had produced a strategic stalemate, which one side could only break through by pouring astronomical sums into new weapons in the hope that its opponent could not match them. The cost to Moscow of such a race would delay any hope of raising the standard of living for ordinary citizens.

At the same time Khruschev had evolved the theory of 'peaceful coexistence and competition'. The best way to win the non-aligned countries to Communism and to strengthen Communist rule within the Soviet block was to overtake the United States economically and industrially.

Because of the nuclear balance, which neither Marx nor Lenin could have foreseen, capitalism would refrain from war. The Communist movement should therefore opt for self-containment and win the battle of coexistence by showing the supremacy of its system.

Khruschev's new policy also presupposed that in accepting peaceful coexistence the West would recognise the status quo of Soviet control in Eastern Europe. And an advanced industrial country like the Soviet Union, as an additional argument for detente, needed to improve its trading relations with the West.

China's interests were different. It did not yet possess nuclear weapons, at least of any significance. It was not a party to any strategic balance enjoyed by the Soviet Union and the United States. It was ringed by American bases and faced the full fury of anti-Communist hostility in the American establishment, where calls for 'preventive nuclear strikes' against China were not uncommon. While feeling more bitter about the United States, China also believed it was invulnerable in the long run even to nuclear attack. Mao is reported to have said that after the Americans had unleashed their hydrogen bombs there would still be 300 million people in China, far more proportionately than there would be in the capitalist countries. In these circumstances Chinese foreign policy had a bravado and unwillingness to compromise quite unlike Khruschev's.

In its relations with the Soviet Union China was becoming bolder. The Chinese revolution had been consolidated. Mao wanted to be consulted on important issues within the Communist movement. He was ambitious for rapid economic development and felt that the more advanced socialist countries, in particular the USSR, should help China to come up to their standard.

But China was a long way from provoking a split within the movement. Indeed, one aspect of its 'tough' line on foreign policy was the view that the Communist movement must preserve its unity. This required a strong leader, which could only be the Soviet Union. Internally there could be no room for revisionism on the Yugoslav model. Externally there must be a firm joint line. It was Khruschev's flirtation with detente, the Chinese thought, that was weakening the camp.

China's first major appearance as a diplomatic factor of importance in the Communist movement was at the conference of Communist parties held in Moscow in November 1957 on the fortieth anniversary of the Russian revolution. Mao attended, and in spite of various compromises between the Soviet and Chinese positions in the final resolutions, it was his conference.

He ensured that in its declaration on intra-Party relations the conference stressed the need for solidarity and mutual fraternal aid. It was lukewarm on the Yugoslav and Polish views in support of the principles of equality, independence and non-interference in internal affairs. In foreign policy Mao shifted the line back to the notion of implacable class war and confrontation between socialism and imperialism.

The conference resolution had little effect on Khruschev's foreign policy. He still hoped for a summit conference with the Americans and a deal in which both sides would accept a measure of peaceful coexistence. They would refrain from provocative attempts to enlarge their sphere of influence. But President Eisenhower would not play. The Soviet overtures for a summit were politely stalled.

In July 1958 the Americans landed troops in the Lebanon during an internal crisis there. The British put troops into Jordan. The Soviet Union saw these moves as aimed against pro-Soviet Governments in Iraq and Egypt. Khruschev reacted with a double appeal—first with another call for a summit meeting, and secondly with a sabre-rattling gesture in the form of an announcement of manoeuvres along the Soviet Union's Middle Eastern frontiers.

Although the crisis blew over, it was apparent that China had not supported Khruschev's policy. It wanted a far more decisive line. At the end of the month Khruschev flew to see Mao to try to patch up the quarrel. The circumstances were very different from his visit to Belgrade in 1955, but his hurried journey to China had something of the same symbolic effect.

It demonstrated that China now had to be consulted on vital issues of policy, emphasised the two countries' differences, and showed that the Soviet Union no longer had the monopoly of leadership. There were now two leading centres in the movement.

Over the next 2 years the argument between the two sides became sharper, even though the issues remained fundamentally the same. Khruschev continued with his summit diplomacy in spite of rising criticism *within the Soviet leadership as well as from the Chinese. By this time the quarrel had inevitably begun to spill over into the rest of the Communist movement.*

Each side was trying to convince the other parties of the validity of its point of view. There had been nothing like this open debate inside the movement since 1927, when Stalin and Trotsky stated their cases before the executive committee of the Communist International (and Trotsky was expelled). In later years rebels were excommunicated without a hearing.

Not only did this new openness increase and intensify the magnitude of the differences between the Soviet Union and China. It also gave a fresh importance to the other Communist parties by according them a kind of juryman's right to judge the movement's leaders. This could only encourage the tendency towards 'national communism' and the open admission of separate political and economic interests.

Albania was the first country to exploit the differences between Moscow and Peking. In 1960 it openly took the Chinese side at the Moscow conference of eighty-one parties. Four years later it was Rumania's turn. The process was subtler than the Albanians'. For several months Rumania sought to mediate between the Soviet Union and China. It succeeded only temporarily, but the net result was to make it easier for Rumania to assert its independence later.

By the end of 1964 the divisions within the movement were visible to all. In Eastern Europe Yugoslavia, Albania and Rumania no longer recognised the Soviet Union's leading role. The dispute between Moscow and Peking could no longer be patched over by a compromise. On the geographical fringes of the movement were two countries, North Vietnam and Cuba, which were trying to keep an uneasy neutrality between the two giants. The era of 'polycentrism' had arrived.

YUGOSLAVIA'S INDEPENDENT LINE

Yugoslavia's lone criticism of the Soviet intervention in Hungary widened the gap between Tito and Khruschev. But there was still room for compromise. Khruschev felt that it would be more dangerous to have Tito outside the Communist movement altogether than to have him within it as an uneasy rebel.

Stalin's attempt at 'excommunication' had been a disaster. It was better to keep the black sheep within the family. Khruschev was realistic enough to see that some of Tito's criticisms of Stalinism had been justified. He, Khruschev, agreed with many of them. Besides, Khruschev and Tito had developed a certain personal affection for each other, and got on well together.

For his part Tito's earlier flirtation with the West had waned a little. The Hungarian uprising had coincided with the combined Anglo-French-Israeli invasion of the Egypt of his great friend Nasser. As a champion of non-alignment in the Third World, Tito saw the West as its main adversary. Now that Khruschev had recognised Yugoslavia's independence—and the Soviet intervention in Hungary did not alter that —Tito felt he could play a part in influencing events in Eastern Europe in the direction of de-Stalinisation. He wanted to reform the system from within, and he still saw Khruschev as the best hope for change inside the Soviet Union.

In the summer of 1957 Tito suggested to Khruschev that they start talking together again. They met in Bucharest in August. Tito promised to recognise East Germany and to come in person to Moscow for the world conference of Communist parties which Khruschev was preparing.

When the draft documents for the conference began circulating, Tito realised the extent of Mao's influence in shaping a tough line both on foreign policy for the Communist movement and, internally, against revisionism. He decided not to attend himself, and the delegation he sent refused to sign the main declaration.

The declaration issued by the twelve Communist parties in Moscow in November 1957 was a compromise. But it leant visibly towards the Chinese point of view. Whereas the Yugoslavs and the Poles would have liked to see an unequivocal statement of each party's independence, the declaration stressed the Soviet Union's leading role.

While it mentioned the principle of state independence, it negated this by saying that 'fraternal mutual aid' (as shown in Hungary in 1956) was essential too. It claimed that in certain circumstances dogmatism (the conservatives' sin) could be more dangerous than revisionism (the reformers' sin), but it emphasised that it was revisionism which tried to undermine socialism, and which was in general 'the main danger at present'. It praised peaceful coexistence but supported Mao's contention

that imperialism rather than socialism had more to fear from war.
Imperialism would 'doom itself to destruction' if it started a war.

24 THE MOSCOW DECLARATION, 1957

. . . The question of war or peaceful coexistence is now the
crucial question of world policy. All the nations must display
the utmost vigilance in regard to the war danger created by
imperialism.

At present the forces of peace have so grown that there is a
real possibility of averting wars, as was demonstrated by the
collapse of the imperialist designs in Egypt. The imperialist
plan to use the counter-revolutionary forces for the overthrow
of the people's democratic system in Hungary has failed as well.

The cause of peace is upheld by the powerful forces of our
era: the invincible camp of socialist countries headed by the
Soviet Union; the peace-loving countries of Asia and Africa
taking an anti-imperialist stand and forming, together with the
socialist countries, a broad peace zone; the international working class and above all its vanguard, the Communist parties; the
liberation movement of the peoples of the colonies and semi-
colonies; the mass peace movement of the peoples; the peoples
of the European countries who have proclaimed neutrality;
the peoples of Latin America and the masses in the imperialist
countries are putting up increasing resistance to the plans for a
new war.

An alliance of these mighty forces could prevent war, but
should the bellicose imperialist maniacs venture, regardless of
anything, to unleash a war, imperialism will doom itself to
destruction, for the peoples will not tolerate a system that
brings them so much suffering and exacts so many sacrifices.

The Communist and workers' parties taking part in the
meeting declare that the Leninist principle of peaceful coexistence of the two systems, which has been further developed
and brought up to date in the decisions of the Twentieth
Congress of the Soviet Communist party, is the sound basis of

the foreign policy of the socialist countries and the dependable pillar of peace and friendship among the peoples. The idea of peaceful coexistence coincides with the five principles advanced jointly by the Chinese People's Republic and the Republic of India and with the programme adopted by the Bandung conference of African-Asian countries. Peace and peaceful coexistence have now become the demands of the broad masses in all countries.

The Communist parties regard the struggle for peace as their foremost task. They will do all in their power to prevent war.

The meeting considers that in the present situation the strengthening of the unity and fraternal co-operation of the socialist countries, the communist and workers' parties and the solidarity of the international working class, national liberation and the democratic movements acquire special significance.

In the bedrock of the relations between the countries of the world socialist system and all the communist and workers' parties lie the principles of Marxism-Leninism, the principles of proletarian internationalism which have been tested by life. Today the vital interests of the working people of all countries call for their support for the Soviet Union and all the socialist countries who, pursuing a policy of preserving peace throughout the world, are the mainstay of peace and social progress. The working class, the democratic forces and the working people everywhere are interested in tirelessly strengthening fraternal contacts for the sake of the common cause, in safeguarding from enemy encroachments the historic political and social gains effected in the Soviet Union—the first and mightiest socialist power—in the Chinese People's Republic and in all the socialist countries, in seeing these gains extended and consolidated.

The socialist countries base their relations on principles of complete equality, respect for territorial integrity, state independence and sovereignty and non-interference in one another's affairs. These are vital principles. However, they do not exhaust the essence of relations between them. Fraternal mutual aid is part and parcel of these relations. This aid is a striking expression of socialist internationalism . . .

Of vital importance in the present stage is the intensified struggle against opportunist trends in the working class and communist movement. The meeting underlines the necessity of resolutely overcoming revisionism and dogmatism in the ranks of the communist and workers' parties. Revisionism and dogmatism in the working class and communist movement are today as they have been in the past international phenomena. Dogmatism and sectarianism hinder the development of Marxist-Leninist theory and its creative application in changing conditions, replace the study of the concrete situation with merely quoting classics and sticking to books and lead to the isolation of the party from the masses. A party that has withdrawn into the shell of sectarianism and that has lost contact with the masses cannot bring victory to the cause of the working class.

In condemning dogmatism, the communist parties believe that the main danger at present is revisionism or, in other words, right-wing opportunism, which as a manifestation of bourgeois ideology paralyses the revolutionary energy of the working class and demands the preservation or restoration of capitalism. However, dogmatism and sectarianism can also be the main dangers at different phases of development in one party or another. It is for each communist party to decide what danger threatens it more at a given time.

It should be pointed out that the conquest of power by the proletariat is only the beginning of the revolution, not its conclusion. After the conquest of power, the working class is faced with the serious tasks of effecting the socialist reconstruction of the national economy and laying the economic and technical foundation of socialism. At the same time the overthrown bourgeoisie always endeavours to make a come-back. The influence exerted on society by the bourgeoisie, the petty bourgeoisie and their intelligentsia is still great. That is why a fairly long time is needed to resolve the issue of who will win—capitalism or socialism. The existence of bourgeois influence is an internal source of revisionism, while surrender to imperialist pressure is its external source.

Modern revisionism seeks to smear the great teachings of Marxism-Leninism, declares that it is 'outmoded' and alleges that it has lost its significance for social progress. The revisionists try to exorcise the revolutionary spirit of Marxism, to undermine faith in socialism among the working class and the working people in general. They deny the historical necessity for a proletarian revolution and the dictatorship of the proletariat during the period of transition from capitalism to socialism, deny the leading role of the Marxist-Leninist party, reject the principles of proletarian internationalism and call for the rejection of the Leninist principles of party organisation and above all of democratic centralism, for transforming the communist party from a militant revolutionary organisation into some kind of debating society . . .

SOURCE: *The New Communist Manifesto and related documents*, edited by Dan N. Jacobs (Evanston, Illinois, 1961)

The conference over, Tito resolved to formulate once again the Yugoslav way to socialism. The resulting work was published in March 1958 as the draft programme for the forthcoming congress of the League of Communists of Yugoslavia. Its content was predictable. It praised workers' councils, condemned bureaucracy and the centralised state, and spoke of the variety of roads to socialism.

To Moscow the document looked like a deliberate and insolent rebuttal of the declaration of the 1957 conference. Khruschev decided to boycott the congress and publish his own rejoinder. On 19 April 1958 the Soviet party's theoretical journal Kommunist *contained a lengthy article rebutting the main points of the draft programme and accusing Yugoslavia of advocating national Communism.*

According to Kommunist *the programme was a departure from the theory and practice of Marxism-Leninism. The Soviet Union did not try, as alleged, to exercise hegemony over other parties. It had not exploited anyone. Most importantly of all, the Yugoslav view that world tension was caused by the existence of the two military blocks, NATO and the Warsaw Pact, was completely false, since only NATO threatened world peace.*

25 Kommunist
MOSCOW'S CRITICISM OF YUGOSLAVIA

It is generally known that the problem of war is rooted in the very essence of imperialism. Nevertheless, the authors of the draft see the main reason of international tension not in the aggressive policy of the imperialist states, but in the existence of the two military political blocks.

All the accusations which the peace-loving peoples justly advance against the imperialist policy of the ruling circles of Western powers, the Draft Programme also ascribes without any grounds to the Socialist countries, using the handy word 'hegemonism' both for the policy of the imperialist and the Socialist states. Can it be said, for instance, that the USSR is conducting a foreign policy which can be classified as a policy of force? Of course not. The policy of force is a policy of preparation for a world war, when a power wants to establish its domination over the world and impose its dictates on other countries, when it endeavors to exploit the world and get super profits for the monopolists. The USSR is conducting a peaceful foreign policy. It has no aggressive or predatory aims. The USSR has no economic motives for seizing foreign territories and plundering other nations. The policy of force grows inevitably from the outlook of the monopolistic bourgeoisie, which holds that force can delay or even annul the operation of objective laws of historical development. This is the creed of a dying way. The USSR bases its policy on Marxism-Leninism, which is alien to the bourgeois idealists' theory of force and which proceeds from objective historical laws stipulating that a dying social system be replaced by another more advanced one.

Objections and resolute protests are evoked by the absolutely groundless deliberations in the Draft Programme as to the so-called divisions into spheres of influence and spheres of interest in which the world's first Socialist power allegedly participates. The Draft states: 'The method of division of spheres of interest and other similar political forms appeared as far back as the conferences of heads of Allied States in Teheran, Yalta and Potsdam, and continued in the postwar period.' In another part of the draft it is said: 'The policy of spheres of interest has poisoned and continues to poison international relations. The peoples of Germany, Korea and Vietnam live in states having two different social systems. They are split by artificial borders and represent smoldering hotbeds of open hostilities.'

It is common knowledge that the USSR was not endeavoring to obtain for itself spheres of interest and spheres of influence in Teheran, in Yalta, or in Potsdam. At these conferences the USSR struggled for the national independence and state sovereignty of the countries of Central and Southeast Europe, never for spheres of its own influence. This was one of the conditions which enabled the peoples of a number of countries liberated from the yoke of Fascism to choose the Socialist path of development.

Dwelling on the achievements in the field of industrialization, the authors of the draft completely ignore the USSR's experience in what is, as far as the dictatorship of the proletariat is concerned, one of the major and most complicated problems of construction of Socialism: the problem of transferring millions of peasants, individual holders, private and petty estates, onto the Socialist path of development. Does this problem not confront all countries which have embarked upon the path of building Socialism? If anyone undertakes to summarize the experience of Socialist construction, how can one ignore the great experience of development of the collective farm system in the USSR?

It must be said that on the whole, the Draft Programme of the League of Yugoslav Communists gives a one-sided description of the historical path covered by the USSR. The draft does not give due consideration to the experience of Socialist construction in the CPR and other people's democracies. It is common knowledge that the experience of the USSR and other Socialist countries has fully confirmed the teaching of Marxist-Leninist theory stating that the processes of Socialist revolution and Socialist construction are based on a number of major laws inherent in all countries embarking upon the path of Socialism.

Unfortunately, the Draft Programme does not devote any space to the general laws of development of Socialism. On the contrary, it concentrates its main attention on the drawbacks and mistakes which the USSR had in the past. These are represented by the authors of the programme as some sort of bureaucratic state tendency.

The implication here is that there is a tendency to turn the state apparatus into a master of society. Under the guise of criticizing alleged attempts at theoretically and ideologically justifying the personality cult, the authors of the draft are accusing Soviet Communists of revising the major points of Marxism-Leninism, primarily in the field of theory of state and law. They write: 'The Marxist-Leninist theory on the dictatorship of the proletariat as a state which withers away, and as a means of struggle of the working class for destroying the economic foundations of capitalism and setting up political and material conditions for a free development of new Socialist relations in society, was turned into Stalin's theory of a state which does not wither away, and which should be made ever stronger in all spheres of social life, and to whose apparatus too much importance is attached in the construction of Socialism, an attitude which sooner or later is bound to obstruct the development of Socialist economic and social factors.'

One can quite definitely say that all these assertions distort the process of development of social life and theoretical thought in the USSR.

Reading the Draft Programme of the League of Communists, one gets the impression that its authors proceeded from an incorrect idea that the state and democracy are incompatible under Socialism. They evidently believe that the development of Socialist democracy is impossible unless the state is abolished and withers away. But that point of view does not correspond to the views of Marxist-Leninism or to the course of social development. One cannot oppose Socialist democracy to the Socialist state and assume that the development of democracy is possible only at the expense of the weakening and withering away of state power. The classics of Marxism-Leninism did not oppose Socialist democracy to the dictatorship of the proletariat, but, on the contrary, held that the dictatorship of the proletariat is precisely the highest form of democracy. It is not by accident that two concepts—to raise the proletariat to the position of a ruling class, and to win the battle of democracy—stand side by side in the manifesto of the Communist Party. This presentation of the question very aptly described the relations between the state and democracy in the period of transition from capitalism to Communism.

The dictatorship of the proletariat is not an ordinary state, not a machine for the suppression of the majority by the minority, as was the case under the dictatorship of the exploiting classes. The classics of Marxism-Leninism said more than once that the dictatorship of the proletariat is no longer a state in the proper meaning of the word, for here the power belongs to the majority of the society, to all the working people. The founders of Marxism saw one of the most important features of the working class state to lie in that it would be a truly democratic state. Emphasizing the inseparable bond of the dictatorship of the proletariat with the popular masses, Marx wrote that this is the transfer of power to the popular masses themselves, which in place of the organized force of their oppression, create their own force . . .

In the Draft Programme, democracy and the battle against bureaucracy are linked up with the withering away of the state. But, of course, it is incorrect to think that the overcoming of bureaucracy and the development of bureaucracy are conceivable only when the state withers away.

The essence of the difference between the point of view of the authors of the draft and the point of view recognized in the international Communist and workers' movement is not in whether or not the principles of equality must be strictly observed. The essence of the difference lies in the fact that in the draft of the programme proletarian internationalism is reduced exclusively to the principles of equality and non-interference in internal affairs, and that the necessity for strengthening the unity and co-operation of the Socialist countries and the Marxist-Leninist Parties is buried in oblivion.

The demand for recognition of the equality of nations is also characteristic of petty-bourgeois nationalism. This nationalism, as Lenin pointed out, declares as internationalism only the recognition of the equality of nations, and purely verbal at that, while it retains national egoism untouched. Lenin explained that when the dictatorship of the proletariat is established in several countries and becomes capable of exerting a decisive influence on the world's politics, the struggle against the deep-rooted petty-bourgeois nationalist prejudices will assume a particularly sharp and burning character. Under certain conditions, proletarian internationalism demands the subordination of the proletarian struggle in one country to the interests of the struggle on a worldwide scale.

Meanwhile, the draft of the programme of the League of Communists of Yugoslavia speaks only about the facts that the relations between the Socialist countries must be based on principles of independence, complete equality and respect for the peculiarities of each individual country. The struggle for the affirmation of these principles in the relations between Socialist countries and proletarian Parties is put forward essentially as the only problem of internationalism, as the supreme aim in relations between the Socialist countries and Socialist movement.

A well-founded question arises: Can the principles of equality and non-interference express the entire essence of relations between the Socialist countries? No, they cannot. The countries

G

in which power is in the hands of the working people, and whose fates are closely interconnected by the community of their social and state systems, interests and aims, build their relations with a strict observance of the principles of equality on the basis of fraternal mutual aid, support and cooperation. Each of them strives to extend all possible aid and support to the fraternal countries in the building of a Socialist society and, at the same time, relies on their help and support. In this, the principle of equality is not violated. Socialist mutual aid essentially excludes the possibility of an advantageous position of some countries at the expense of others. On the contrary, it contributes to the common development, to the fullest possible unfolding of the material and spiritual forces for each people forming part of the Socialist community, and to the consolidation of the power of this community as a whole.

The authors of the Draft Programme of the League of Communists of Yugoslavia are trying to back up their one-sided understanding of proletarian internationalism by reference to a presumable violation of Socialist principles in the relations between the Socialist countries. 'In practice,' they write, 'it has turned out that, either because of strong international political positions or because of the different degrees of economic development, it is possible that one Socialist country maintains by various means its unequal relations with another or several other Socialist countries.'

The draft actually defends national Communism which, as is well known, lays emphasis on the special national features in the building of Socialism, and rejects that which is most important and universally significant that has been revealed by the experience of all Socialist countries. The criticism of the ideas of national Communism is declared in this document to be a result of dogmatic or chauvinistic egoistic conceptions or a result of ideological influences or intrigues of the bourgeoisie.

SOURCE: *Kommunist* (19 April 1958), translated in *The Soviet-Yugoslav Controversy*, op cit

In spite of the firm arguments in the Kommunist *article, its tone remained basically amicable. It was the Chinese rather than Moscow who decided to take things further. They accused Tito of abandoning socialism.*

In response to Mao's initiative Khruschev for a time took a harder line himself. In May he suspended the £100 million loan which he had promised Yugoslavia. In a speech in Sofia he claimed that during the Hungarian uprising the Yugoslav embassy in Budapest had been a centre of subversion.

Yet the underlying trend was still for the Soviet-Yugoslav rapprochement begun by Khruschev in 1955 to continue. In the great Sino-Soviet dispute that had started to develop Tito favoured the Soviet side. The policy of peaceful coexistence which Khruschev was now advocating was precisely the one which Tito himself had long supported.

Unlike his neighbours Rumania and Albania, Tito had no need to exploit the differences between Moscow and Peking. His independence was tolerably secure. For all their ups and downs Belgrade and Moscow under Khruschev developed the best example of a mature relationship between two different versions of socialism which there had, and indeed still has, yet been. The fundamental split of 1948 was far enough back in the past for it to be accepted as part of the landscape. Inter-governmental relations were separated from inter-party ones. The two sides agreed to differ ideologically while maintaining a normal diplomatic dialogue.

ALBANIA AND CHINA BREAK AWAY

The Albanian break with Moscow preceded the public split between the Soviet Union and China by 2 years. It remains one of the strangest episodes of postwar European history. How could a tiny backward Balkan country dare to abuse the most powerful state in the Communist world, and then switch its allegiance to China, thousands of miles away?

To find the main reason one must go back to the beginnings of Albanian communism. The party was founded on 8 November 1941—by two Yugoslavs. This strange anomaly explains a good deal. In the wartime partisan struggle against the Nazis and the Italians Tito needed allies. He welded the handful of local Albanian communists into a party and a guerrilla movement.

One problem was the future of the Kosmet, the area of prewar Yugoslavia peopled largely by Albanians. In 1940 the Yugoslav communists had promised to return it to Albania if they came to power. But during the war Tito changed his mind and decided to keep it.

After the war Tito went further. He proposed to incorporate the whole of Albania as a constituent republic of the Yugoslav Federation. The move caused a fierce split in the Albanian party leadership. On the one hand, Koci Xoxe, the deputy prime minister, minister of the interior, and secretary of the central committee, agreed with the plan. On the other hand there were the Albanian nationalists who resented being a client state of Yugoslavia and wanted independence. Theirs was the first example of national Communism from a ruling party.

Yugoslav-Albanian relations were an almost exact replica of Soviet relations with its smaller brethren in Eastern Europe. Joint Yugoslav-Albanian companies were set up. There was to be a customs union. Serbo-Croat was a compulsory subject in Albanian schools. The Yugoslav party represented the Albanians at Cominform meetings.

The Albanian issue became a major factor in Stalin's dispute with Tito, Enver Hoxha, the party leader, keeping close contact with Moscow. Stalin used the issue as a way of bringing pressure to bear on Yugoslavia. He was worried at the prospect of a Balkan Federation of Yugoslavia and Bulgaria which would be communist but independent of Moscow. To undermine Yugoslavia was an obvious move.

Xoxe was preparing for a rapid incorporation or 'unification' of Albania with Yugoslavia. When the Yugoslavs made plans to send two army divisions into Albania with his agreement (see Document 6), Stalin forced through his own break with Yugoslavia. Hoxha, who was a nationalist, immediately broke with Yugoslavia, too, abrogated the various bilateral treaties and purged Xoxe.

Anti-Yugoslav feeling in Albania was strong. It helped to cement Hoxha's control over the country. Tito became a hated figure. The Soviet Union was Albania's protector. It sent enormous amounts of aid to help to industrialise the country.

Against this background Khruschev's reconciliation with Tito in 1955 obviously came as a source of deep concern to Enver Hoxha. He now saw the prospect of his protector getting together with his arch-enemy.

While adopting a façade of agreeing with Khruschev's new policy of de-Stalinisation, Hoxha desperately resisted the pressures, passed on from Tito to Khruschev, for a rehabilitation of Yugoslavia's ally, Xoxe, who had been executed a few months after his arrest in 1948.

The Hungarian uprising and the consequent cooling of relations between Moscow and Belgrade saved Hoxha for a time. But he saw that the basis for long-term Soviet-Yugoslav rapprochement was strong. He started to cast around for an alternative protector, and found one in China.

Like Mao, Hoxha became fierce in his attacks on Tito's 'revisionism'. Like Mao, he took a hard line against Khruschev's notion of peaceful coexistence. As the signs of independence grew, Khruschev flew to Tirana in May 1959 to try to restore good relations. His visit was a disaster. He advised the Albanians against rapid industrialisation, and encouraged them to end their quarrel with Yugoslavia. The Albanian leaders were furious. Mehmet Shehu, the Prime Minister, told Mikoyan later: 'Stalin made two mistakes. First he died too early, and second he failed to liquidate the entire present Soviet leadership.'

The next year the row became visible to the rest of the movement for the first time. Khruschev used the occasion of the Rumanian party congress in June 1960 to circulate a document criticising Chinese policy. At a closed meeting he condemned Mao's 'adventurism'. The Albanian delegate supported the Chinese position, and accused Khruschev of 'putsch-like' tactics in rounding on the Chinese unexpectedly and without warning.

Khruschev tried to bully the Albanians back into line. In the middle of a food shortage caused by drought that summer, he suddenly cut back on Soviet aid. He encouraged a pro-Soviet faction within the Albanian leadership to attempt a coup d'état. The move failed.

Hoxha's response was to prepare a blistering denunciation of Khruschev, which he planned to make in front of the combined delegates of the eighty-one communist and workers' parties due to meet in Moscow in November. A final series of meetings between Hoxha and Khruschev in Moscow shortly before the conference produced no solution. On 16 November Hoxha took the stand at the conference in a closed session and delivered the most astonishing attack on a top Soviet party leader by a supposed ally which has ever been made. Delegates gasped as Hoxha rebuked Khruschev for holding revisionist and anti-Marxist views, and recounted his various threats against the Albanian leadership. The highpoint was the story of the famine when Khruschev, according to Hoxha, preferred to feed Soviet mice rather than starving Albanians.

Maurice Thorez, the French Communist party leader commented after the speech: 'The members of our delegation listened to the speech with a feeling of shame. As militant communists they have never heard such language either in their party meetings or in the meetings of the international communist party . . .'

26 Enver Hoxha
ALBANIA DENOUNCES KHRUSCHEV

As the draft-statement which has been prepared emphasises, our socialist camp is much stronger than that of the imperialists. Socialism rises higher and stronger day by day while imperialism grows weaker and decays. We would make use of all our means and exert all our efforts to speed up this process. This will come about if we abide loyally and unwaveringly by Marxism-Leninism and apply it correctly. Otherwise, we will retard this process, for we have to cope with a ruthless enemy-imperialism, headed by U.S. imperialism whom we must defeat and destroy.

We want peace, while imperialism does not want peace and is preparing for a third world war. We must fight with all our might to avert a world war and to bring about the triumph in the world of a just and democratic peace. This will come about when imperialism will have been forced to disarm. Imperialism will not disarm of its own free will. To believe anything of the kind is merely to deceive oneself and others. Therefore we should confront imperialism with the colossal economic, military, moral, political and ideological strength of the socialist camp, as well as with the combined strength of the peoples throughout the world. We should sabotage by every means the war which the imperialists are preparing.

The Albanian Workers' Party has neither kept nor will it

ever keep secret from its people this situation and threat from imperialism menacing peace-loving mankind. We can assure you that the Albanian people, who detest war, have not been alarmed by this correct action of their Party: they have not become pessimistic nor have they been marking time as far as socialist construction is concerned. They have a clear vision of the future and have set to work with full confidence, being always on guard, keeping the pick in one hand and the rifle in the other. We hold the view that US-led imperialism should be mercilessly exposed politically and ideologically. At no time should we permit flattery, prettification or softness towards imperialism. No concessions of principle should be made to imperialism. Tactics and compromises on our part should help our cause, and not that of the enemy.

A lot is said about peaceful coexistence. Some even go so far as to assert such absurdities as that People's China and Albania are allegedly opposed to peaceful coexistence. Obviously, such harmful and erroneous views should be rejected once and for all. There can be no socialist state, there can be no Communist who is opposed to peaceful coexistence, who is a warmonger.

Great Lenin was the first to put forward the principle of peaceful coexistence among states of different social orders as an objective necessity as long as socialist and capitalist states exist side by side in the world. Standing loyal to this great principle of Lenin's, our Albanian Workers' Party has always held and still holds that the policy of peaceful coexistence responds to the vital interests of all the peoples, and responds to the purpose of the further consolidation of the positions of socialism; therefore, this principle of Lenin's is the basis of the entire foreign policy of our people's state.

Peaceful coexistence between two opposing systems does not imply, as the modern revisionists claim, that we should give up the class struggle. On the contrary, the class struggle must continue; the political and ideological struggle against imperialism, against bourgeois and revisionist ideology, should become even more intense. In our persistent struggle to establish Leninist peaceful coexistence while making no concessions of principle to imperialism, we should further promote the class struggle in capitalist countries as well as the national-liberation movement of the people of colonial and dependent countries ...

There may be comrades who reproach us Albanians with being stubborn, hot-blooded, sectarian, dogmatic and what not, but we reject all these false accusations and tell them that we do not deviate from these positions for they are Marxist-Leninist positions.

They say that we are in favor of war and against coexistence. Comrade Kozlov [Khruschev's close colleague] has even put to us, Albanians, these alternatives: either coexistence, as he conceives it, or an atomic bomb from the imperialists, which will turn Albania into a heap of ashes and leave no Albanian alive. Until now, no representative of U.S. imperialism has made such an atomic threat against the Albanian people. But here it is and from a member of the Presidium of the Central Committee of the Communist Party of the Soviet Union and to whom? To a small heroic country, to a people who have fought, through centuries, against savage and innumerable enemies and who have never bent the knee, to a small country and to a people who have fought with unprecedented heroism against the Nazis and Italian fascists, to a people who are bound like flesh to bone to the glorious Soviet Union, to a party which abides loyally, consistently and to the last by Marxism-Leninism and by the Communist Party of the Soviet Union. But Comrade Frol Kozlov, you have made a mistake; you cannot frighten us into yielding to your wrongly calculated wishes and we never confound the glorious party of Lenin with you who behave so badly, with such shamelessness towards the Albanian people and towards the Albanian Workers' Party ...

We think that the Bucharest conference did a great disservice to the cause of the international communist movement ... The aim was to have the Chinese Communist Party condemned by the movement for faults which do not exist and are baseless ...

Right from the start, when the Soviet comrades began their feverish and impermissible work of inveigling the comrades, on our delegation to Bucharest, it became clear that the Soviet comrades wished to lead the delegation of the Albanian Workers' Party into the trap they had prepared, to bring them into line with the distorted views of the Soviet comrades . . .

In October this year, Comrade Khruschev declared solemnly to the Chinese comrades, 'We will treat Albania like Yugoslavia'. We say this at this meeting of international communism so that all may see how far things have gone and what an attitude is being taken towards a small socialist country. What 'crime' has the Albanian Workers' Party committed for our country to be treated like Tito's Yugoslavia? Have we by any chance betrayed Marxism-Leninism as Tito's clique has done? Or did we break away from the camp and hitch up with U.S. imperialism as revisionist Yugoslavia has done? No, and all the international communist movement, all the concrete political, ideological and economic activity of our Party and our State during these 16 years since the liberation of the country bear testimony to this . . .

Our only 'crime' is that in Bucharest we did not agree that a fraternal communist party like the Chinese Communist Party should be unjustly condemned; our only 'crime' is that we had the courage to oppose openly, at an international communist meeting (and not in the market place) the unjust action of Comrade Khruschev, our only 'crime' is that we are a small Party of a small and poor country which, according to Comrade Khruschev, should merely applaud and approve but express no opinion of its own. But this is neither Marxist nor acceptable. Marxism-Leninism has granted us the right to have our say and we will not give up this right for anyone, neither on account of political and economic pressure nor on account of the threats and epithets that they might hurl at us . . .

No, Comrade Khruschev, you continue to blunder and hold very wrong opinions about our Party. The Albanian Workers' Party has its own views and will answer for them both to its own people as well as to the international communist and workers' movement.

We are obliged to inform this meeting that the Soviet leaders have in fact passed from threats to treating Albania in the same way as Titoite Yugoslavia, to concrete acts. This year our country has suffered many natural calamities. There was a big earthquake, the flood in October, and especially the drought which was terrible, with not a drop of rain for 120 days in succession. Nearly all the grain was lost. The people were threatened with starvation. The very limited reserves were consumed. Our government urgently sought to buy grain from the Soviet Union, explaining the very critical situation we were faced with. This happened after the Bucharest Meeting. We waited 45 days for a reply from the Soviet Government, while we had only 15 days bread for the people. After 45 days and after repeated official requests, the Soviet Government, instead of 50,000 tons, accorded us only 10,000 tons, that is enough to last us 15 days, and this grain was to be delivered during the months of September and October. This was open pressure on our Party to submit to the wishes of the Soviet comrades.

During these critical days we got wise to many things. Did the Soviet Union, which sells grain to the whole world, not have 50,000 tons to give the Albanian people who are loyal brothers of the Soviet people, loyal to Marxism-Leninism and to the socialist camp, at a time when, through no fault of their own, they were threatened with starvation? Comrade Khruschev had once said to us: 'Do not worry about grain, for all that you consume in a whole year is eaten by mice in our country.' The mice in the Soviet Union might eat but the Albanian people could be left to die of starvation until the leadership of the Albanian Workers' Party submits to the will of the Soviet leaders. This is terrible comrades, but it is true. If they hear about it, the Soviet people will never forgive them, for it is neither Marxist-Leninist, internationalist, nor humane . . .

The fact that Albania proceeds along the path of socialism and that it is a member of the socialist camp is not determined by you, Comrade Khruschev, it does not depend on your wishes. This has been determined by the Albanian people headed by their Albanian Workers' Party, by their struggle and there is no force capable of turning them from that course.

As regards your claim that our Workers' Party is the weakest link in the socialist camp and the international communist movement, we say that the twenty-year history of our Party, the heroic struggle of our people and our Party against the fascist invaders and the sixteen years that have elapsed since the liberation of the country to this day, during which period our small Party and our people have faced up to all the storms, show the contrary. Surrounded by enemies like an island amidst the waves, the People's Republic of Albania has courageously withstood all the assaults and provocations of the imperialists and their lackeys. Like a granite rock it has held and holds high the banner of socialism behind the enemy lines. You raised your hand, Comrade Khruschev, against a small country and its Party, but we are convinced that the Soviet people who shed their blood in defense of our people, also, that the great Party of Lenin are not in agreement with this activity of yours. We have full confidence in Marxism-Leninism, we are certain that fraternal parties which have sent their delegates to this meeting will size up and pass judgment on this issue with Marxist-Leninist justice . . .

SOURCE: Enver Hoxha's speech, delivered in Moscow on 16 November 1960, from *The Albanian Workers' Party in Battle with Modern Revisionism: Speeches and Articles* (Tirana 1972)

After Hoxha's speech relations between Moscow and Tirana were near breaking point. Khruschev recalled all the Soviet aid specialists from Albania at the beginning of 1961. The Soviet and East European credits promised for the Five-year plan up to 1965 were cancelled. Soviet submarines left their bases in the Adriatic port of Vlore.

Khruschev still drew the line at outright excommunication of Albania, mainly because this would have meant confronting the Chinese, who were openly sympathising with Enver Hoxha. They had promised to send Chinese aid to replace the cancelled Soviet consignments. However, on the eve of the Soviet party's Twenty-second Congress the Albanians despatched a cheeky letter to the Soviet central committee criticising the 'crude, anti-Marxist activity of N. Khruschev and his group'. Khruschev decided to expose the Albanians at the Congress.

On 17 October 1961 he denounced them publicly. Pravda *printed his speech the following day. It was an historic moment—the first public attack on another communist party since the Yugoslavs were expelled from the Cominform in 1948. Some observers take it as the first formal admission of the Sino-Soviet split, for the Albanians were a kind of proxy for the Chinese. In holding up the correctness of his policies and the falseness of the Albanians', Khruschev was really speaking to Mao Tse-Tung.*

27 Nikita Khruschev
ATTACK ON THE ALBANIANS

Comrades! Events show our party's foreign policy line, framed at the Twentieth Congress to have been correct. Keeping to this line, we have scored major victories. And although our strength has now grown substantially, we shall pursue the Leninist course just as unswervingly and consistently, seeking to make the idea of peaceful coexistence prevail. Present conditions have opened up the prospect of achieving peaceful coexistence over the entire period within which the social and political problems now dividing the world must be resolved. Matters are reaching a point where even before the total victory of socialism on earth while capitalism holds on in part of the world, there will be a real chance of eliminating war from the life of society.

V. I. Lenin taught us to remain firm, unyielding, and uncompromising where fundamental positions of principle are at stake. Under the most trying circumstances when the only socialist state was withstanding the assaults of the whole capitalist world, when the enemy was attacking us at the front, in the rear and on the flanks, Vladimir Ilyich used firm and resolute language with the imperialists, at the same time pursuing a flexible line and constantly retaining the initiative.

What are the tasks for Soviet foreign policy growing out of the present international situation? We must continue: unswervingly and consistently implementing the principle of the peaceful coexistence of states with different social systems, as the general course of the Soviet Union's foreign policy;

strengthening the unity of the socialist countries on the basis of fraternal co-operation and mutual assistance, and doing our part to reinforce the might of the world socialist system;

developing contacts and co-operating with all fighters for peace throughout the world; joining all who want peace in a stand against those who want war;

strengthening proletarian solidarity with the working class and working people of the whole world, giving all possible moral and material support to peoples who are struggling for their liberation from imperialist and colonial oppression and for the consolidation of their independence;

developing international business ties, economic co-operation, and trade on the broadest possible scale with all countries which want to maintain such relations with the Soviet Union;

carrying on a vigorous and flexible foreign policy, striving to secure settlement of urgent world problems through negotiations, exposing intrigues and manoeuvres of the warmongers, and establishing businesslike co-operation with all states on the basis of reciprocity.

Experience has proved that the principle of peaceful co-existence of states with different social systems, a principle put forward by the great Lenin, represents the way to preserve peace and prevent a global war of annihilation . . .

Comrades! The Twentieth Congress, by condemning the cult of the individual which is alien to the spirit of Marxism-Leninism, opened a broad vista for the creative forces of the party and the people and furthered the expansion and strengthening of the party's ties with the people and the

increasing of its combat readiness . . . As it later turned out, our
party's policy of overcoming the harmful effects of the cult of
the individual did not meet with due understanding from the
leaders of the Albanian Workers' Party: indeed, they began to
conduct a struggle against this policy.

Everyone knows that until recently the relations between the
Soviet Union and the People's Republic of Albania and between
the Communist Party of the Soviet Union and the Albanian
Workers' Party were friendly and good. The peoples of our
country gave Albania comprehensive, disinterested help in
developing its economy and in socialist construction. We
sincerely wanted and want to see Albania a flourishing socialist
republic and its people happy and enjoying all the benefits of
the new life.

For many years the Albanian leaders signified their complete
unity of views with the central committee of our party and the
Soviet Government on all questions of the international Communist movement . . . The facts show however that recently the
Albanian leaders, despite their former declarations and the
decisions of their own party congress, have sharply changed
their course without any excuse and have taken the path of an
acute deterioration of relations with our party and with the
Soviet Union. They began to depart from the commonly
agreed line of the whole world Communist movement on the
major questions of our times, something which became particularly obvious from the middle of last year.

Now the Albanian leaders do not conceal the fact that they
do not like the course our party has taken of firmly overcoming
the harmful consequences of the Stalin cult, of sharply condemning the abuse of power, and of restoring Leninist norms
of party and state life. Evidently the Albanian leaders in their
hearts disagreed with the conclusions of the 1957 and 1960
conferences of fraternal parties, which, as everybody knows,
approved the decisions of the Twentieth Congress and our
party's policy. This stand by the Albanian leaders is explained
by the fact that they themselves, to our regret and distress, are

repeating the methods that occurred in our country in the period of the cult of the individual.

We are following events in Albania with a feeling of anxiety for the destinies of the heroic Albanian people. We are pained to see that rank-and-file Albanian Communists and the whole Albanian people, who are vitally interested in friendship and co-operation with all the socialist countries are obliged to pay for the mistaken line of the Albanian leaders. We are deeply troubled by this situation and have persistently sought and are seeking ways of overcoming the differences that have arisen.

The course drawn up by the Twentieth Congress of the Party is a Leninist course, and we cannot concede on this fundamental question to either the Albanian leaders or anyone else. To depart from the Twentieth Congress line would mean not heeding the danger of the appearance of the Stalin cult even when it was in embryo. It would mean disregarding the costly lessons of history, forgetting the price that our party paid for not having heeded in time the instructions of its great leader.

Now the Albanian leaders are trying to pull our party back to ways that they like but which will never be repeated in our country. Our party will continue firmly and unswervingly to carry out the line of its Twentieth Congress, a line that has withstood the test of time. No-one will succeed in diverting us from the Leninist path.

If the Albanian leaders hold dear the interests of their people and the cause of building socialism in Albania, if they really want friendship with the CPSU and all the fraternal parties, they should renounce their mistaken views and return to the path of unity and close co-operation in the fraternal family of the socialist commonwealth, the path of unity of the whole international Communist movement . . .

SOURCE: Speech by N. S. Khruschev at the Twenty-second Congress of the CPSU, in *Pravda* (18 October 1961), translated in *Current Soviet Policies*, IV, the documentary record of the

Twenty-second Congress of the Communist Party of the Soviet Union, edited by Charlotte Saikowski and Leo Gruliow; from *The Current Digest of the Soviet Press*. Translation Copyright 1973 by *The Current Digest of the Soviet Press*, published weekly at the Ohio State University by the American Association for the Advancement of Slavic Studies; reprinted by permission of the *Digest*

Khruschev's speech was a clear challenge to China. Throughout the simmering Soviet-Albanian dispute China's criticism of Khruschev's foreign policies had not abated. Khruschev's visit to Peking in August 1958 had produced no easing of tension between the two parties. The year 1959 was no better. The Soviet Union unilaterally revoked its agreement to share nuclear technology with China.

At the end of the year during the border war between India and China Khruschev refused to take sides, much to the annoyance of Peking. After his ebullient tour of the United States, which also left the Chinese sour, the Soviet party leader made a last visit to Peking. But the meeting ended fruitlessly, without even a communiqué.

The situation deteriorated still further in 1960. Khruschev's attack on the Chinese at the closed sessions of the Rumanian congress in June was followed by his decision in August to withdraw all the Soviet advisers from China and to cancel many of the two countries' agreements.

The three-week conference of eighty-one communist and workers' parties in Moscow in November was meant to produce a public compromise between Moscow and Peking, which it did—in spite of Hoxha's extraordinary speech and subsequent walk-out. But underneath the differences only grew wider. During the spring and summer of 1961 Khruschev in private documents began to accuse the Chinese leadership of 'disloyalty' and 'incitement to world war'.

In October Chou En-Lai came to Moscow for what was to be his last appearance at a Soviet party congress. After Khruschev's denunciation of the Albanians Chou felt he had no alternative but to reply with a speech deploring the attack, and accusing Khruschev of not adopting a serious, Marxist-Leninist approach. He later ostentatiously laid a wreath on Stalin's tomb and left Moscow early.

28 Chou En-Lai
A REBUKE FOR KHRUSCHEV

... We hold that if, unfortunately, disputes and disagreements have arisen among the fraternal parties and fraternal countries, we should resolve them patiently, being guided by the spirit of proletarian internationalism and by the principles of equality and the achievement of unanimity through consultation.

Open unilateral condemnation of a fraternal party does not make for unity, does not help to settle issues. Openly exposing disputes between fraternal parties and fraternal countries for enemies to see cannot be regarded as a serious, Marxist-Leninist approach. Such an approach can only pain friends and gladden foes.

The Communist party of China sincerely hopes that the fraternal parties between which the disputes and disagreements exist will reunite on the basis of Marxism-Leninism and on the basis of mutual respect for independence and equality. I think that this is the position that we Communists should take on this question ...

SOURCE: *Pravda* (20 October 1961), translated in *Current Soviet Policies*, IV, the documentary record of the Twenty-second Congress of the Communist Party of the Soviet Union, edited by Charlotte Saikowski and Leo Gruliow; from *The Current Digest of the Soviet Press*. Translation Copyright 1973 by *The Current Digest of the Soviet Press*, published weekly at the Ohio State University by the American Association for the Advancement of Slavic Studies; reprinted by permission of the *Digest*

In 1962 the Sino-Soviet dispute continued to worsen. In 1963 it came into the open. In preparation for bilateral talks to be held in Moscow, the Chinese published their position in a long letter to the Soviet party on 14 June 1963. It contained twenty-five theses on Communist strategy and was the clearest statement of Mao's views.

H

For the first time the Chinese repudiated the Soviet Union's pre-eminence as leader of the Communist movement. Ironically, after 1956, it was Mao who opposed 'national Communism' most strongly and encouraged the Soviet Union to exercise firm leadership. Now his position had reversed.

Exactly 10 years after Stalin's death the Communist world had split into two. There were now two pretenders to leadership. This struggle was unlike that between Stalin and Trotsky for the prevailing influence over one country. It was a struggle between two major parties at the head of two powerful countries for the leadership of the whole 'socialist camp'.

29 THE CHINESE LETTER

Dear Comrades,

The Central Committee of the Communist Party of China has studied the letter of the Central Committee of the Communist Party of the Soviet Union of 30 March, 1963.

All who have the unity of the socialist camp and the international communist movement at heart are deeply concerned about the talks between the Chinese and Soviet Parties and hope that our talks will help to eliminate differences, strengthen unity and create favourable conditions for convening a meeting of representatives of all the Communist and Workers' Parties.

It is the common and sacred duty of the Communist and Workers' Parties of all countries to uphold and strengthen the unity of the international communist movement. The Chinese and Soviet Parties bear a heavier responsibility for the unity of the entire socialist camp and international communist movement and should of course make commensurately greater efforts.

A number of major differences of principle now exist in the international communist movement. But however serious these differences, we should exercise sufficient patience and find ways to eliminate them so that we can unite our forces and strengthen the struggle against our common enemy . . .

The Moscow Meetings of 1957 and 1960 adopted the Declara-

tion and the Statement respectively after a full exchange of
views and in accordance with the principle of reaching unanimity through consultation. The two documents point out
the characteristics of our epoch and the common laws of
socialist revolution and socialist construction, and lay down the
common line of all the Communist and Workers' Parties. They
are the common programme of the international communist
movement . . .

What are the revolutionary principles of the Declaration
and the Statement? They may be summarised as follows:

Workers of all countries, unite; workers of the world, unite
with the oppressed peoples and oppressed nations; oppose
imperialism and reaction in all countries; strive for world peace,
national liberation, people's democracy and socialism; consolidate and expand the socialist camp; bring the proletarian
world revolution step by step to complete victory; and establish
a new world without imperialism, without capitalism and without the exploitation of man by man.

This, in our view, is the general line of the international
communist movement at the present stage.

This general line proceeds from the actual world situation
taken as a whole and from a class analysis of the fundamental
contradictions in the contemporary world, and is directed
against the counter-revolutionary global strategy of U.S.
imperialism.

This general line is one of forming a broad united front, with
the socialist camp and the international proletariat as its
nucleus, to oppose the imperialists and reactionaries headed by
the United States; it is a line of boldly arousing the masses,
expanding the revolutionary forces, winning over the middle
forces and isolating the reactionary forces.

This general line is one of resolute revolutionary struggle by
the people of all countries and of carrying the proletarian world
revolution forward to the end; it is the line that most effectively
combats imperialism and defends world peace.

If the general line of the international communist movement is one-sidedly reduced to 'peaceful coexistence', 'peaceful competition' and 'peaceful transition', this is to violate the revolutionary principles of the 1957 Declaration and the 1960 Statement, to discard the historical mission of proletarian world revolution, and to depart from the revolutionary teachings of Marxism-Leninism . . .

The following erroneous views should be repudiated on the question of the fundamental contradictions of the contemporary world:

(a) the view which blots out the class content of the contradiction between the socialist and the imperialist camps and fails to see this contradiction as one between states under the dictatorship of the proletariat and states under the dictatorship of the monopoly capitalists;

(b) the view which recognizes only the contradiction between the socialist and the imperialist camps while neglecting or underestimating the contradictions between the proletariat and the bourgeoisie in the capitalist world, between the oppressed nations and imperialism, among the imperialist countries and among the monopoly capitalist groups, and the struggles to which these contradictions give rise;

(c) the view which maintains with regard to the capitalist world that the contradiction between the proletariat and the bourgeoisie can be resolved without a proletarian revolution in each country and that the contradiction between the oppressed nations and imperialism can be resolved without revolution by the oppressed nations;

(d) the view which denies that the development of the inherent contradictions in the contemporary capitalist world inevitably leads to a new situation in which the imperialist countries are locked in an intense struggle, and asserts that the contradictions among the imperialist countries can be reconciled, or even eliminated, by 'international agreements among the big monopolies'; and

(e) the view which maintains that the contradiction between the two world systems of socialism and capitalism will automatically disappear in the course of 'economic competition', that the other fundamental world contradictions will automatically do so with the disappearance of the contradiction between the two systems, and that a 'world without wars', a new world of 'all-round co-operation', will appear.

It is obvious that these erroneous views inevitably lead to erroneous and harmful policies and hence to setbacks and losses of one kind or another to the cause of the people and of socialism . . .

It is under new historical conditions that the Communist and Workers' Parties are now carrying on the task of proletarian internationalist unity and struggle. When only one socialist country existed and when this country was faced with hostility and jeopardized by all the imperialists and reactionaries because it firmly pursued the correct Marxist-Leninist line and policies, the touchstone of proletarian internationalism for every Communist Party was whether or not it resolutely defended the only socialist country. Now there is a socialist camp consisting of thirteen countries, Albania, Bulgaria, China, Cuba, Czechoslovakia, the German Democratic Republic, Hungary, the Democratic People's Republic of Korea, Mongolia, Poland, Rumania, the Soviet Union and the Democratic Republic of Viet Nam. Under these circumstances, the touchstone of proletarian internationalism for every Communist Party is whether or not it resolutely defends the whole of the socialist camp, whether or not it defends the unity of all the countries in the camp on the basis of Marxism-Leninism and whether or not it defends the Marxist-Leninist line and policies which the socialist countries ought to pursue.

If anybody does not pursue the correct Marxist-Leninist line and policies, does not defend the unity of the socialist camp but on the contrary creates tension and splits within it, or even follows the policies of the Yugoslav revisionists, tries to liquidate the socialist camp or helps capitalist countries to attack fraternal socialist countries, then he is betraying the interests of the entire international proletariat and the people of the world . . .

Over the past few years, certain persons have violated
Lenin's integral teachings about the interrelationship of leaders,
party, class and masses, and raised the issue of 'combating the
cult of the individual'; this is erroneous and harmful.

The theory propounded by Lenin is as follows:

(a) The masses are divided into classes;

(b) Classes are usually led by political parties;

(c) Political parties, as a general rule, are directed by more
or less stable groups composed of the most authoritative,
influential and experienced members, who are elected to the
most responsible positions and are called leaders.

Lenin said, 'All this is elementary.'

The party of the proletariat is the headquarters of the
proletariat in revolution and struggle. Every proletarian party
must practise centralism based on democracy and establish
a strong Marxist-Leninist leadership before it can become an
organized and battle-worthy vanguard. To raise the question
of 'combating the cult of the individual' is actually to counterpose the leaders to the masses, undermine the Party's unified
leadership which is based on democratic centralism, dissipate
its fighting strength and disintegrate its ranks.

Lenin criticized the erroneous views which counterpose the
leaders to the masses. He called them 'ridiculously absurd and
stupid.'

The Communist Party of China has always disapproved of
exaggerating the role of the individual, has advocated and
persistently practised democratic centralism within the Party
and advocated the linking of the leadership with the masses,
maintaining that correct leadership must know how to con-
centrate the views of the masses.

While loudly combating the so-called cult of the individual,
certain persons are in reality doing their best to defame the
proletarian party and the dictatorship of the proletariat. At
the same time, they are enormously exaggerating the role of
certain individuals, shifting all errors on to others and claiming
all credit for themselves.

What is more serious is that, under the pretext of 'combating the cult of the individual', certain persons are crudely interfering in the internal affairs of other fraternal Parties and fraternal countries and forcing other fraternal Parties to change their leadership in order to impose their own wrong line on these Parties. What is all this if not great-power chauvinism, sectarianism and splittism? What is all this if not subversion?

SOURCE: 'The CCP's Proposal Concerning the General Line of the International Communist Movement' (14 June 1963), published in the *Peking Review*, VI, 25 (21 June 1963); reprinted in *The Sino-Soviet Rift*, edited by William E. Griffiths (1964)

RUMANIA OPPOSES COMECON

Rumania's break with the Soviet Union, when it came, was based mainly on economic considerations and on differences between Bucharest and Moscow over where Rumania's national interests lay. But the first signs of tension were ideological.

After consolidating his position in the Soviet Union, Khruschev decided to encourage the old Rumanian leader Gheorghe Gheorghiu-Dej, like his counterparts in the other 'people's democracies', to initiate political reforms. Gheorghiu-Dej was a master tactician. In April 1954 in line with Moscow's wish for collective leadership he gave up the post of first secretary of the party and stayed on as prime minister. A year later he switched back, making himself first secretary and giving the premiership to a trusted colleague. Then he put all the blame for the excesses in the postwar period on to the group led by Anna Pauker, who had been purged from the Politburo in 1952.

As had happened with the Polish party, too, the wartime experience had left deep divisions among Rumania's communists. There were three groups: those who had spent the war in Moscow, many of them Jews; those who were in the underground resistance at home; and those (a small number in Rumania but more in Poland) who were in the West. Anna Pauker's group were mainly 'Muscovites'. Gheorghiu-Dej replaced them with 'Rumanians'. They became the architects of the country's later independent line. In the meantime under their leadership de-Stalinisation in Rumania meant little more than the renaming of various streets that had been called after Stalin.

The crunch with the Soviet Union came over the economy. Rumania had followed the Soviet model in industrialising rapidly and in the 1950s achieved one of the fastest growth rates in the whole of Eastern Europe. The country had considerable natural wealth—oil, natural gas, bauxite, copper, coal and hydroelectric potential.

With the setting up of the Common Market in Western Europe in 1957 Khruschev resolved to turn the Council for Mutual Economic Assistance (Comecon), Eastern Europe's economic organisation, into a general body for joint international planning and specialisation. Comecon had been established in 1949 but had remained largely an organisation on paper only. Now it was to take wings. Under the international division of labour, countries would only produce what was most economic for them. The most developed countries, East Germany and Czechoslovakia, were moderately keen on the idea although they had some suspicions that integration might mean they should hold back their own growth to allow the more backward countries to catch up. They argued that they should remain the main industrial states in Eastern Europe while others provided raw materials and agricultural products.

From 1958 onwards the idea of Comecon integration was raised periodically but it was not until 1961 that Khruschev put it forward systematically. In the following June a meeting of Eastern Europe's party leaders agreed to set up an executive committee to coordinate planning in Comecon.

Rumania saw the programme as a political and economic threat. Three years earlier Khruschev had suggested to the Albanians that they abandon industrialisation and turn the country into 'a flowering garden'. The Albanians refused. A similar invitation was now being made to the Rumanians, but with the difference that a supranational planning body was envisaged which would have the power to override a single country's objections.

As an economic proposition Khruschev's idea had much to recommend it. A rational division of labour would help to prevent duplication, allow for mass production, and ensure that countries used their particular endowments to the best advantage. But Khruschev's proposal foundered on Rumania's understandable mistrust. It also went against the grain of the ideology of all-out industrialisation which the Soviet Union hitherto had always recommended. Nor was there any guarantee that the more advanced countries in Comecon would help to bring up the other countries to their level. On the contrary, all the signs were that the gap between them would grow wider.

Shortly after the Comecon summit in June 1962 Khruschev spelt out his scheme for supranational planning in the theoretical journal Kommunist.

30 Nikita Khruschev
ON SUPRANATIONAL PLANNING

The socialist countries are now at a stage when the conditions have ripened for raising their economic and political co-operation to a new and higher level. At this level a special significance is acquired by co-ordinated national economic plans, the socialist division of labour, and by the co-ordination and specialisation of production. This will guarantee the successful organic development of the socialist countries.

The socialist world system is now at a stage when it is no longer possible to correctly chart its development by merely adding up the national economies. The task now is to do everything to consolidate the national economy of each country, to broaden its relations and gradually advance towards that single world-wide organism embracing the system as a whole which Lenin's genius foresaw . . .

By co-ordinating the economies of the socialist countries we will be able to increase tenfold the strength of each of them and of the system as a whole . . . Streamlining the system of co-operation and mutual aid will help to bring the socialist nations closer, make for the evening-up of their economic development generally and at the same time enhance the sovereignty of each country since each will have in addition to its own forces the support of the entire socialist community . . .

Division of labour between countries has existed for a long

time. The advance made by the productive forces of society is indissolubly associated with it. Capitalism, as we know, made the widest possible use of the international division of labour right from its inception. But under capitalism the link between the economies of the different countries took on a deformed, lop-sided character with the result that in the imperialist era the world found itself so divided that alongside a small group of highly-developed countries, which were exploiters, there was a large number of underdeveloped countries which became the objects of colonial exploitation and dependence.

Under capitalism the international division of labour serves as an instrument for the monopolies to plunder nations whose economic development was retarded. Through a thousand economic threads including financial and other 'aid', these countries were bound to the big powers, thus deepening their inequality and dooming millions to backwardness and poverty.

Under socialism the international division of labour is a striking expression of the relations of genuine friendship, equality and co-operation that exist between the nations building the new life . . . It is aimed at abolishing the economic gap between the industrial countries and the formerly backward countries, at facilitating the industrialisation of the agrarian countries, at accelerating their economic and cultural progress, at consolidating the independence of all the socialist countries . . . The various economies, supplementing one another, will gradually merge into a single streamlined economic complex with each having its own place and functions and in which each country, each people will have an even stronger foundation for solving the national tasks of socialist construction . . .

Marx pointed out that under capitalism planning was possible only within the limit of a single enterprise, beyond the walls of which reigned the spontaneous action of economic laws and anarchy of production. We Communists, having abolished capitalist relations in our countries, have got rid of the anarchy of production and at national levels have curbed blind market relations. Now we are confronted with the need to go beyond this, and by starting out from planning on a national scale go in for planning at the level of the Council for Mutual Economic Assistance, and afterwards at the level of the socialist world system as a whole.

Our aim is to build the socialist world economy as a single entity. But to accomplish this we have no resources to draw on other than the accumulations created by each. It follows then that we cannot get on without agreement, even if only in general outline, on the policy of creating and utilising accumulations on the scale of the Council. This presupposes, first, allocating funds for building common enterprises—a thing which we have just begun to do—and secondly agreed national investment plans which would take into account both the national and the common interests . . .

Since our job is to secure the most effective use of the means allocated for capital building, it may well be that we shall have to switch some of the allocations from country to country, on mutually acceptable conditions of course for the interested countries. This way of doing things will be well worthwhile and will benefit the countries concerned . . .

SOURCE: 'Vital Questions of the Development of the Socialist World System', by N. S. Khruschev, published in *Kommunist* (September 1962), translated in the *World Marxist Review*, Vol 5, no 9

With the publication of Khruschev's article the Rumanians saw that he meant business. They decided that the best way to resist Moscow was to take the issue to the nation. 'National Communism' is an apt phrase for Rumania's policy. For the first time since they had come to power the party leaders systematically went out to win popular backing, and the ground they chose was traditional nationalism. Meetings were held up and down the country where party spokesmen explained the dispute with Comecon.

Rumania's two sticking points were the threat to their further industrialisation, and Comecon's wish to move away from the unanimity principle towards a majority voting procedure in the executive committee. This would mean a country could no longer have a veto over decisions by the rest of the membership. In theory it would thus lose control over decisions affecting its national interests.

The Rumanians were quick to see that the best way to emphasise and strengthen their desire for independence would be to use the growing Sino-Soviet dispute. Throughout the winter of 1962–3 they began to break away from the policy of the rest of the Soviet camp. They published no newspaper articles attacking Peking, increased their trade with China and sent their ambassador back to Albania. The Chinese reciprocated. In their famous public letter to the Soviet party (see Document 29) they criticised the idea of supranational integration. The other East European Communist parties refused to publish the Chinese letter. The Rumanians did not.

Bucharest's resistance was successful. Other Eastern European leaders also had their doubts about the integration scheme, but the Rumanians' stand was undoubtedly the main factor which led Khruschev reluctantly to drop the plan in July 1963.

But the Rumanians went on with the defiance, though now in the political field. The most striking sign of their new position came with their bold attempt at the end of 1963 to mediate between Moscow and Peking. They wrote to both sides appealing for an end to public polemics to allow private talks to have a chance of settling the two Communist giants' differences. The move produced a temporary lull in the public propaganda campaign emanating from the Soviet and Chinese capitals, but no concrete improvement. As the Sino-Soviet split widened, Khruschev pressed Gheorghiu-Dej to join the Soviet side. He consistently refused, and even went so far as to boycott Khruschev's seventieth birthday celebrations in Moscow in the spring of 1964.

A week later an enlarged plenary meeting of the central committee published a resolution which has since become known as Rumania's 'Declaration of Independence'. In it the Rumanians asserted their ideological sovereignty—'Nobody can decide what is and what is not correct for other parties'. They proudly quoted Lenin for the view that national distinctions would continue for a very long time even during the building of socialism. It was the most sophisticated definition of national Communism ever made.

31 Rumanian Communist Party
RUMANIA'S DECLARATION OF INDEPENDENCE

Co-operation within CMEA [Comccon] is achieved on the basis of the principles of fully equal rights, of the observance of national sovereignty and interests, of mutual advantage and comradely assistance. As concerns the method of economic co-operation, the socialist countries which are members of CMEA have established that the main means of achieving the international socialist division of labour and the main form of co-operation between their economies is to co-ordinate plans on the basis of bilateral and multilateral agreements. During the development of co-operative relations, various forms and measures have been suggested, such as a joint plan and a single planning body for all member countries, inter-state technical and production units, enterprises jointly owned by several countries, inter-state economic complexes and so on.

Our party has very clearly expressed its point of view, declaring that since the essence of the suggested measures lies in shifting some functions of economic management from the competence of the respective states to that of super-state bodies, these measures are not in keeping with the principles underlying relations between the socialist countries. The idea of a single planning body for all CMEA countries has the most serious political and economic implications. The planned management of the national economy is one of the fundamental, essential and inalienable attributes of the sovergeinty of the socialist state— the state plan being the chief means through which the socialist state achieves its political and socio-economic objectives, establishes the directions and rates of development of the national economy, its fundamental proportions, the accumulations, the measures for raising the people's living standards and cultural level. The sovereignty of the socialist state requires that it effectively and fully avails itself of the means for the practical implementation of these attributes, holding in its hands all the levers of managing economic and social life. Transmitting such levers to the competence of super-state or extra-state bodies would turn sovereignty into a meaningless notion . . .

Lenin's words are fully valid when he said that 'as long as there are national and state distinctions among peoples and countries—and such distinctions will continue for a very long time even after the establishment of the proletarian dictatorship on a world scale—the unity of the communist movement does not require the elimination of diversities or the abolition of national distinctions (which would be an absurd dream at present), but the implementation of the fundamental principles of communism'.

Starting from this Leninist truth, the socialist countries achieve their unity of action in all fields, economic as well as political, by reciprocal consultation, the joint elaboration of common stands on the major issues of principle, and not by setting up exclusive solutions by some super-state authority. This is the only correct and possible way of developing co-operation among sovereign and equal states . . .

The experience won by the countries of the world socialist system has verified the need to take into account the general laws of socialist construction which have universal validity. These laws have an objective nature and it is clearly impossible for anyone arbitrarily to 'create' new general laws or to proclaim that specific individual phenomena have universal value, or to try to impose them upon other countries and in different historical conditions. The requirements of these laws are applied to concrete conditions of great diversity, in keeping with the level or stage of each socialist country's development and its historical peculiarities . . .

In establishing the best forms and methods of building socialism, the Communist and Workers' parties take into account both the objective laws and the concrete historical conditions prevailing in their own countries. They carry on an intense creative activity, grasping the requirements of social development, synthesising their own experience and studying that of fraternal countries . . . There are not and there cannot be any unique patterns and recipes. Nobody can decide what is and what is not correct for other countries and parties. It is up to every Marxist-Leninist party. It is a sovereign right of each socialist state to elaborate, choose or change the forms and methods of socialist construction . . .

SOURCE: Rumanian Party Statement (26 April 1964), translated in the BBC Monitoring Service's Summary of World Broadcasts, EE/1539/C/1; reprinted by permission of the BBC

PART FOUR

The Quiet Years and Their Sudden End

At the end of 1964 Nikita Khruschev was ousted from power. His zigzags in foreign policy, the dangerous impetuosity he displayed over the Cuban missile crisis in 1962, the failure of his agricultural policy, his grandiose but disastrous plans for Comecon, uneasiness that he might be pushing de-Stalinisation too far—all these factors led to his colleagues' gradual resentment of him reaching breaking point.

There followed a quiet period of consolidation throughout Eastern Europe. In the Soviet Union the new triumvirate of Brezhnev, Kosygin and Podgorny needed time to make their mark. Their attitude towards the 'people's democracies' was more relaxed, and, as it turned out, was sounder. They contained the threat of national communism by not provoking quarrels or forcing through attempts at changes.

Inside the Soviet Union their attention was turned towards economic reform. By the early 1960s a group of Soviet economists was already arguing that the country must go over to 'intensive' rather than 'extensive' methods of raising production. Ways of cutting costs, of modernising, and of installing new machinery of the right kind in the right place had to replace simple reliance on massive investments and the growth of the labour force.

In Eastern Europe a similar debate was going on. The phase of rapid industrialisation was coming to an end. Crude accumulation and investment in heavy industry were no longer enough to sustain high growth rates.

Between 1960 and 1962 growth rates fell in nearly all the Comecon countries. In Czechoslovakia in 1963 output itself declined slightly from the level of the previous year. The only three countries which continued to expand rapidly between 1960 and 1962 were the most backward countries—Albania, Bulgaria and Rumania. Gradually the other Comecon nations turned towards various forms of economic reform. By 1967 every country except Poland had either launched a reform or was on the point of doing so.

The general trend was to reduce the amount of central control over the economy and to allow more room for private enterprise and initiative at the margin. In agriculture the Party abandoned its hostility to the idea of peasants having private allotments. Partly in order to increase agricultural production and partly to stop the drift of people from the villages into the towns, more investment was earmarked for the countryside. Government credits were made available for fertilisers, for tractors, and for mechanisation. In the service sector the Party offered a new deal to small-scale private craftsmen, artisans, and repairmen.

As long as the commanding heights of the economy were under state control the Party felt it was ideologically safe to allow private traders to operate at the fringes. Even in Czechoslovakia, which by the early 1960s had nationalised every shop and workshop in the country, the Government started to issue licences for private craftsmen to open up again.

In the economy as a whole the reforms led to a decentralisation of state control, more chance for enterprises to dispose of their profits as they wished, and a widening of income differentials with the aim of encouraging skilled workers and technicians.

By themselves the reforms contained no political dynamite. They were not liberalising measures so much as attempts at increasing efficiency and modernisation. In two countries only did the issue of reform produce a crisis. In Poland Gomulka ruled it out, and his refusal helped to precipitate an upheaval. In Czechoslovakia the economic reform was linked to wider political and ideological changes.

ATTEMPTS AT REFORM

Already under Khruschev Soviet economists had begun to suggest that profits should be given a greater role as an indicator of economic efficiency.

I

The first article to appear on these lines was written by Prof Evsei Liberman and came out on 9 September 1962 in Pravda. *But it was not until 1965 that the idea became official policy.*

In September of that year at a plenary meeting of the central committee the Soviet Prime Minister, Alexei Kosygin, launched a new system of management. Enterprises would keep a larger share of the profits they earned. Out of this they could pay increased bonuses to their staff or finance capital investments. The number of central directives which every enterprise was bound to follow was reduced. Better use was to be made of 'such important levers as profit, prices, bonuses, and credits', as the central committee resolution put it.

In January the Government had announced that about 400 consumer goods factories would go over to a system of production based on demand. Textile and leather factories, for example, would take orders from clothing and shoe manufacturers who themselves would be working to retailers' specifications.

Some Western observers misinterpreted the reform as 'a return to capitalism'. Prompted by an article in Time *magazine which featured him on the front cover, Prof Liberman explained the purpose of the reform in the journal* Soviet Life.

32 Evsei Liberman
PROFITS IN THE SOVIET UNION

There is nothing new in the use of profits in the Soviet Union. Our enterprises have been making profits in money form for more than forty years, ever since 1921. It is with these profits that we have built up our giant industrial potential, thanks to which we have moved to a leading position in world science and technology. And we have accomplished this without major longterm credits from other countries.

Why has the question of profits been so widely discussed in the Soviet Union lately? Not because profits did not exist before and are only now being introduced. The reason is that profit was not, and still is not, used as the major overall indicator of the efficient operation of our enterprises. Besides profit, we have been using a fairly large number of obligatory indicators—among others, gross output, assortment, lower costs, number of employees, size of payroll, output per employee, and average wages. The multiplicity of indicators hamstrung the initiative of the enterprises. Their main concern often was to turn out as great a volume of goods as possible since they would be rated chiefly on gross output. Furthermore, enterprises did not pay much attention to how they used their assets. Trying to meet their output quotas in the easiest way for themselves, they asked for and received free from the state a great deal of plant which they did not always use efficiently or to full capacity. How do we explain that?

For a long time the Soviet Union was the only socialist country. We stood alone, surrounded by a world in which there were many who wanted to change our social system by force. We had to build up our own industries and secure our defences at all costs and in the shortest possible time. Such considerations as the quality and appearance of goods, or even their cost, did not count. This policy completely justified itself. The Soviet Union not only held its own in the war of 1941–1945 but played the decisive role in saving the world from fascism. That was worth any price. And that was our 'profit' then.

But, as Lenin often said, our virtues if exaggerated can turn into vices. And that is what happened when we held to the same administrative methods of economic management after we entered the stage of peaceful economic competition with the industrial countries of the West.

We want to give every citizen, not only the well-to-do, a high standard of living, in the intellectual as well as the material sense . . . Before we can bring people's intellectual capacities to full flower we must first satisfy their material needs, place goods and services of high quality within everyone's reach. These needs must be satisfied, moreover, with the lowest possible production outlays and the fullest possible utilisation of all assets.

All this cannot be done with the old methods of administrative direction and centralised management. We must change over to a system whereby the enterprises themselves have a material incentive to provide the best possible service to the consumer. It is clear that to do this we must free the enterprises from the excessive number of obligatory indicators. In my opinion, the criteria for rating the work of enterprises should be: first, how well they carry out their plans of deliveries (in actual products); and if these plans are fulfilled then second, their level of profitability. I believe that out of their profits enterprises should have to pay into the state budget a certain percentage of the value of their assets as 'payment for use of plant'. The purpose would be to spur enterprises to make the most productive use of their assets. Part of the remaining share of the profits would go into incentive pay system funds, the amount depending on the level of profitability. The rest of the profits would accrue to the state budget to finance the expansion of production and to satisfy the welfare needs of the population.

Why do I choose profit as the indicator? Because profit generalises all aspects of operation, including quality of output. The prices of better articles have to be correspondingly higher than those of articles that are outmoded and not properly suited to their purpose. It is important to note however that profit in this case is neither the sole nor the chief aim of production. We are interested above all in products with which to meet the needs of the people and of industry. Profit is used merely as the main generalising and stimulating indicator of efficiency, as a device for rating the operation of enterprises.

Yet Western press comments on my writings blare away about the term 'profit', very often ignoring the fact that the title of my *Pravda* article of 9 September 1962 was 'The plan, profits and bonuses'. They make a lot of noise about profit but say nothing about planning.

Actually my point is to encourage enterprises, by means of bonuses from profits, to draw up good plans, that is plans which are advantageous both to themselves and to society. And not only to draw them up but carry them out, with encouragement from profits. It is not a question of relaxing (or rejecting) planning but on the contrary of improving it by drawing the enterprises themselves first and foremost into the planning process, for the enterprises always know their real potentialities best and should study and know the demands of customers . . .

Under socialism profits can be a yardstick of production efficiency to a far greater degree than in the West, for in the Soviet Union profits follow in principle only from technological and organisational improvement. This also means that profits here will play an important but subsidiary role, like money in general, and not the main role. After providing a yardstick of production achievement and a means of encouraging such achievement, profits in the Soviet Union are used wholly for the needs of society. They are returned to the population in the form of social services and expanded production, which guarantees full employment and better and easier working conditions for everyone . . .

SOURCE: *Soviet Life* (July 1965)

Hungary's economic reform began somewhat later, on 1 January 1968. More radical than its Soviet counterpart, it allowed for considerable variations in the field of prices. This was an attempt to bring production into a closer relationship with the consumer and to ascertain real costs. A three-tier system of prices was set up.

Some prices were fixed, some were completely free to be raised or lowered as factory managers saw fit, and some could fluctuate within centrally imposed limits. Enterprises producing intermediate goods were also able to decide on the prices they charged to other factories. The rest of the reform followed the decentralising features already adopted in the Soviet Union.

The overall aim of the 'new economic mechanism', as it came to be called, was to bring market pressure to bear on inefficient industries. Firms which could not modernise or cut costs enough or hold prices down would find themselves running to the state for subsidies. The Government made it clear that it would not back them indefinitely. Some firms would have to close down and their workers would be helped to find new employment. In the language most commonly used by Eastern European economists Hungary needed to go over to an 'intensive' form of development in which growth had to be concentrated in the most modern and efficient sectors.

In a lecture given 2 years after the reform began Rezsoe Nyers, a member of the Politburo and the reform's main initiator, described the background to it. He concluded that if anything the reform had been launched a little late.

33 Rezsoe Nyers
HUNGARY'S SLOW ADVANCE

In analysing post-liberation economic progress we have to distinguish the stage of reconstruction from the period of development. Though an extremely fast growth rate is possible in the stage of reconstruction as the national economy approaches an income level already attained earlier, the period of development aims to attain a new, higher income level.

In Hungary we lived through a longish period of reconstruction from 1945 to 1950. War damage, tremendous losses in fixed assets and a fall in production were made up for. The pace of reconstruction was swift, especially after 1947 when the first three-year plan was launched. Hungary went through another period of reconstruction later, in the years 1957–58, when the decline caused by the counter-revolution [the official description of the 1956 events] had to be overcome. That was also successfully done. It should be noted however that even successful reconstruction must not be mistaken for expansion, since in the meantime the economy underwent only relative development; taking a longterm view the results of reconstruction are not visible nor do they appear in statistics.

The period of development can thus be reckoned from 1950, when the transformation of the economic structure was initiated at the same time with the establishment of socialist productive relations and the two measures jointly resulted in speeding up the growth of national income. The average annual growth of national income in the inter-war years was below 2 per cent. Between 1950 and 1968 it rose to nearly 6 per cent, that is to say, it grew three times as fast as during the Horthy era. On a comparative basis one can say that Hungary developed more rapidly in the past twenty years than the capitalist countries but more slowly than the majority of socialist countries. Considering the last ten years, however, Hungary kept level with the development rate of the countries of the Council for Mutual Economic Assistance . . . The largest source of income before the liberation was agriculture. Since then industry has taken the lead . . .

During the last twenty years the value of both real incomes and consumption rose two and a half times. This is a substantial rise as compared with developments in the past, even if we consider that it was achieved in a period when the share of investments increased considerably. In 1938, in the Hungary of old, only 7 per cent of national income was allocated to investment. As a result development was slow. In 1950 this share was raised to 18 per cent. In the early 1950s moreover, those in charge raised it above a feasible level which had to be given up because of the economic disproportions produced. Since 1957 the share of investments has been about 24 to 28 per cent and that of consumption about 70 to 74 per cent . . .

If we look at twenty years of economic progress in Hungary in order to find out whether or not we have come closer to the production level of the most advanced capitalist countries, we can say that Hungary certainly has done so, in respect of the volume and organisation of production, thanks to taking advantage of the way society is organised. In terms of employment and social services we have surpassed most capitalist countries.

In the field of labour productivity, enterprise organisation and per capita consumption, the twenty-years-old gap still separates Hungary from the most highly developed capitalist countries. Hungary has not fallen back, but neither has it lessened the gap. The fact of the matter is that although national income in Hungary has grown faster, yet development was of necessity extensive, with a slower rise in the productivity of labour compared to the most advanced capitalist countries . . . I wish to emphasise that extensive development cannot be regarded as a mistake. At most it can be said that the switch-over to the intensive method was a little slower than necessary. If we wanted to discuss major mistakes then we ought to speak about the unrealistic notions of the early fifties and the negative aspects of the 'zigzag period'.

SOURCE: 'Problems of Profitability and Income Distribution', by Rezsoe Nyers, published in the *New Hungarian Quarterly*, Vol XI (Budapest 1970)

Of all the Eastern European economies Czechoslovakia's reached the profoundest state of crisis. In 1962 production actually dropped, a rare feat in any country. One reason was that Czechoslovakia had a more sophisticated industrial economy than its neighbours and thus felt the declining usefulness of a centralised command economy earlier.

By January 1965 Ota Sik, an economist and member of the central committee, had persuaded his colleagues to prepare for reform. He explained the need for it, and the faults of the old system in an article in the journal Problems of Peace and Socialism. *Although his argument was similar to that of Nyers in Hungary (see Document 33), his language was tougher and more uncompromising.*

34 Ota Sik
THE LEGACY OF CENTRAL PLANNING

Czechoslovakia's economic progress since the liberation and the establishment of people's democratic government is clear proof of the advantages of socialism. The national income in 1963 rose to 260 per cent of the 1937 level with industrial output increasing 4·8-fold. From the completion of postwar reconstruction, as a result of the fulfilment of the 1947–48 two-year plan, the average annual rate of growth of national income up to 1960 was 8 per cent, and of industrial production 11·6 per cent.

As the building of socialism progressed, the standard of living rose considerably, workers' real wages rising in 1963 to 164 per cent of the prewar level. The industrial potential of socialist Czechoslovakia substantially exceeded that of the prewar bourgeois republic, which already then ranked among the industrially developed countries.

But the comparatively rapid rate of growth notwithstanding, the emphasis on extensive rather than intensive development resulted in a lag in efficiency. It was necessary to expand production facilities, to build new capacities and enlarge the old, and to bring more manpower into industry. But for all that the exhaustion of the extensive sources of output growth made it imperative to turn to intensive development for the sources of greater efficiency which the existing system of planning and management had failed to reveal. By the sixties the economy, together with the continued lag in efficiency, began to lose its dynamic quality. It became obvious that the existing system of management could not ensure the necessary radical and lasting upswing in the economy.

There are times, in particular the transition from capitalist to socialist economy, when strict centralised management is necessary. Centralisation helped us to accelerate the social and structural re-moulding of the economy and to ensure progress along socialist lines at a time when the class composition of the managerial personnel underwent a radical change and it facilitated rapid equalisation of the economic levels in the various parts of the country. But as socialist economic development gradually got into its stride, rigid centralised planning and management became the main impediments to greater efficiency . . .

By setting the enterprises quantitative tasks through directives, they prompted them primarily to increase output measured in terms of gross or marketable production or by similar yardsticks. This frequently led to enterprises using funds or materials uneconomically, to lack of co-ordination in the production of certain items and to the unjustified import of raw materials and other items. Both in an economic and administrative respect the supplier plants were in a privileged position in relation to the buyer plants. They could press their goods on them whether they were actually needed or not. The one-sided drive for more output was accompanied by a lack of sufficient stimuli to improve technology, to go over to the use of new materials and turn out better and more up-to-date goods. This slackening in the qualitative sphere was, broadly speaking the result of obsolete methods of management . . .

SOURCE: 'Czechoslovakia's New System of Economic Planning and Management', by Ota Sik, published in *Otazky Miru a Socialismu*, no 3 (1965). English translation in *Eastern European Economics* (1965)

If economic reform provided the major subject for debate inside the party, outside it the issue of de-Stalinisation was still strong. The technical, scientific, and professional intelligentsia could feel that in the economy at least greater use would be made of experts. But what could the literary and cultural intelligentsia rejoice over?

The first decade since the dictator's death had produced enormous changes from the ending of crude police terror and 'the cult of the personality' to a more realistic attitude to political developments. But it was still unclear what the limits of reform were in the arts, or in literature. How much criticism and self-criticism would the party allow? How serious were its protestations about preventing a repetition of Stalinism?

In 1961 at the Twenty-second Congress of the Communist Party of the Soviet Union Khruschev had given a new boost to the de-Stalinisation campaign. Stalin's body was taken out of the mausoleum in Red Square where it had lain alongside Lenin, and was buried by the Kremlin wall. Every town, village, and square called after him was renamed. It now seemed that Khruschev had recovered from the setback caused by the Polish and Hungarian events of 1956, which had led him to slow down or even reverse the trend towards liberalisation in the Soviet Union and elsewhere.

The Twenty-second Congress not only revived the issue but seemed to take it further. The debate about Stalin was allowed to proceed outside the party. In 1962 Khruschev authorised the publication of Alexander Solzhenitsyn's One Day in the Life of Ivan Denisovich.

For the first time in the Soviet Union a work appeared which depicted the catastrophic human effect of Stalin's terror. Solzhenitsyn himself had served for long periods at the front during World War II and was twice decorated. In early 1945 he was arrested and charged with making derogatory remarks about Stalin. He spent the next 8 years in labour camps. After Stalin's death he was released but had to spend another 3 years away from central Russia in exile.

The book's hero Ivan Denisovich Shukhov was also sent, unjustly, to a Siberian camp. In graphic detail Solzhenitsyn describes the grim conditions and the haphazard way, typical of a dictatorship, in which he was sent there.

35 Alexander Solzhenitsyn
STALIN'S LABOUR CAMPS EXPOSED

According to his dossier Ivan Denisovich Shukhov had been sentenced for high treason. He had testified to it himself. Yes, he'd surrendered to the Germans with the intention of betraying his country and he'd returned from captivity to carry out a mission for German intelligence. What sort of mission neither Shukhov nor the interrogator could say. So it had been left at that—a mission.

Shukhov reckoned simply. If he didn't sign, he'd be shot. If he signed he'd still get a chance to live. So he signed.

But what really happened was this. In February 1942 their whole army was surrounded on the north-west front. No food was parachuted to them. There were no planes. Things got so bad that they were scraping the hooves of dead horses—the horn could be soaked in water and eaten. They'd no ammunition left. So the Germans rounded them up in the forest, a few at a time. Shukhov was in one of these groups, and remained in German captivity for a day or two. Then five of them managed to escape. They stole through the forest and marshes again, and, by a miracle, reached their own lines. A tommy-gunner shot two of them on the spot, a third died of his wounds, but two got through. Had they been wiser they'd have said they'd been wandering round the forest, and then nothing would have happened. But they told the truth: they said they were escaped P.O.W's. P.O.W's, you fuckers! If five of them had got through, their statements could have been found to tally and they might have been believed. But with two it was hopeless. You've put your bloody heads together and cooked up that escape story, they were told.

Deaf though he was, Senka caught on that they were talking about escaping from the Germans, and said in a loud voice:

'Three times I escaped and three times they caught me.'

Senka who had suffered so much was usually silent: he didn't hear what people said and didn't mix in their conversation. Little was known about him, only that he'd been in Buchenwald, where he'd worked with the underground and smuggled in arms for the mutiny: and how the Germans had punished him by tying his wrists behind his back, hanging him up by them, and flogging him.

'You've been in for eight years, Vanya,' Kilgas argued. 'But what camps? Not 'specials'. You had women to sleep with. You didn't wear numbers. But try and spend eight years in a 'special'—doing hard labour. No-one's come out of a special alive.'

'Women! Logs, not women.'

Shukhov stared at the coals in the stove and remembered his seven years in the north. And how he worked for three years hauling logs—for packing cases and sleepers.

The flames in the camp fires had danced up there, too—at timber-felling during the night. Their chief made it a rule that any team that had failed in its quota had to stay in the forest after dark.

They'd toil back to the camp in the early hours but had to be in the forest again next morning.

'N-no, brothers . . . I think we have a quieter life here,' he lisped. 'Here, when the shift's over, we go back to the camp whether our stint's done or not. That's a law. And bread— a hundred grammes more, basic, than up there. Here a man can live. All right, it's a 'special' camp. So what? Does it bother you to wear a number. They don't weigh anything, those numbers.'

'A quieter life, d'you call it?', Fetiukov hissed. (The dinner was getting near and everyone was huddling round the stove.) 'Men having their throats cut, in their bunks! And you call it quieter!'

'Not men—squealers.' Pavlo raised a threatening finger at Fetiukov.

True enough, something new had started up. Two men, known to be squealers, had been found in their bunks one morning with their throats cut . . .

SOURCE: *One Day in the Life of Ivan Denisovich*, by Alexander Solzhenitsyn, first published in *Novy Mir* (Moscow 1962). Translated by Ralph Parker. English translation Copyright © 1963 by E. P. Dutton & Co, Inc, New York, and Victor Gollancz, Ltd, London. Published in the USA by E. P. Dutton & Co, Inc, and used with their permission

Solzhenitsyn's story encouraged the authorities in other countries to publish a spate of similar works. Writers now felt free to write about subjects that had previously been taboo, or to bring out of their desks manuscripts which they had not dared to reveal before. Authors launched themselves on a wave of introspective literature about Stalinism, about the guilt of ordinary citizens in having let it happen, and about the rash idealism of the early postwar period which had made people blind or insensitive to the horrors that followed.

Consciences which had kept quiet for years could now speak again. As François Fejtö wrote later in the 'History of the People's Democracies', 'one had the impression in reading the best works and seeing the most striking films of the Eastern countries that their creators are being driven

by an irresistible force making them act as witnesses in a vast, unique trial, the trial of socialism betrayed, of faith scoffed at, of conscience violated.'

In 1965 Khruschev's successors decided the process had gone far enough. Even under Khruschev the publication of One Day in the Life of Ivan Denisovich *turned out to be an exception and no other book of comparable power appeared in the Soviet Union. But several Soviet authors published books abroad under pseudonyms but with impunity.*

In September 1965 the Soviet authorities arrested two of these authors, Andrei Sinyavsky and Yuli Daniel. They were among the most prominent authors to have written about Stalinism. They were charged with having illegally sent manuscripts abroad to be published there under pseudonyms. Sinyavsky and Daniel admitted the truth of the charges but denied that the works were anti-Soviet. After the flimsiest of arguments the court decided otherwise, and Sinyavsky was sentenced to 7 years' and Daniel to 5 years' hard labour. The sentences aroused protests around the world, including several from Western Communists.

36 Yuli Daniel
FINAL PLEA

I knew that I should have the right of making a final plea and I wondered whether I should waive this right altogether, as I am entitled to, or whether to limit myself to the usual generalities. But then I realised that this is not only my last word at this trial but perhaps the last word that I shall be able to say to people in my life. And there are people here, there are people sitting in the courtroom, and there are also people sitting on the bench. It is for this reason that I decided to speak.

In the final plea of my comrade Sinyavsky there was a note of despair about the impossibility of breaking through a blank wall of incomprehension and unwillingness to listen. I am not so pessimistic. I wish to go over the arguments of the prosecution and the defence once again.

Throughout the trial I kept asking myself: what is the purpose of questioning us? The answer should be obvious and simple: to hear our replies and then put the next question, to conduct the hearing in such a way as finally to arrive at the truth.

This has not happened. To make my point clear I will remind you once again of the way things have gone. I shall talk only about my own works—I hope my friend Sinyavsky will forgive me, he talked about both of us—it is simply that I remember my own things best.

I was asked all the time why I wrote my story 'This is Moscow speaking'. Every time I replied: 'Because I felt there was a real danger of the resurgence of the cult of personality'. To this the answer was always 'What is the relevance of the cult of personality, if the story was written in 1960–61?' To this I said 'It was precisely in these years that a number of events made one feel that the cult of personality was being revived.'

This was not denied. I was not told 'You are lying. This is not true'. My words were simply ignored as though I had never said them. Then the prosecution would say 'You have slandered your people, country, and Government by your monstrous invention about "Public Murder Day".'

To this I replied: 'It could have happened—one has only to think of the crimes committed in the days of the cult of personality; they are far more terrible than anything written by me or Sinyavsky.' At this point the prosecution stopped listening, did not reply to me and simply ignored what I had said. This refusal to listen to what we were saying, this deafness to all our explanations, was characteristic of the whole of this trial.

It was the same story with another of my works. Asked why I had written 'Atonement', I explained: 'Because I think that all the members of a society, each of us individually and all of us collectively, are responsible for what happens.' It may be that I am wrong or that this is a fallacy, but all the prosecution said was: 'This is a slander on the Soviet people and the Soviet intelligentsia.' They did not argue with me, they simply paid no attention to what I was saying. 'Slander' was the easiest reply to anything said by the defendants . . .

SOURCE: The opening passage of Yuli Daniel's final plea at his trial comes from *On Trial*, the case of Sinyavsky (Tertz) and Daniel (Arzhak), a transcript of the trial proceedings edited by Leopold Labedz and Max Hayward (1967)

Apart from individual victims like those described by Solzhenitsyn, a number of entire nationalities suffered under Stalin's rule. During the war seven ethnic groups, totalling some $1\frac{1}{2}$ million people, had been deported to Central Asia. This was done either as a punishment for, or to prevent, collaboration with the Nazis who were advancing towards the Volga and the Caucasus.

One of the worst legacies of Stalinism was the snail-like pace at which rehabilitation was granted to these groups. In his secret speech at the Twentieth Party Congress (Document 13) Khruschev mentioned these deportations in his list of Stalin's crimes. In the following year decrees were passed reconstituting the autonomous territories of the Kalmuks, the Chichen-Ingush, the Karachay and the Balkars. Many members of these nationalities had fought alongside Soviet troops and their repatriation was a belated gesture of recognition that their history was not as black as Stalin had claimed.

The treatment of two other groups—the Volga Germans and the Crimean Tatars—was different. Khruschev did nothing for them. Finally in 1964 the Germans were rehabilitated. The Tatars' turn came in 1967 but neither nationality was allowed to go back to its native lands. Those who tried to return were evicted by force.

Remarkably, in spite of this persecution, a number of Crimean Tatars resolved to protest. For the first time for many years Soviet citizens began to take public and collective action in pursuit of their claims, either by sit-down demonstrations, by petitions, or protests outside courtrooms. It was this activity that gave the Tatars their wider significance, and alerted the world to the start of an amorphous but determined protest movement inside the Soviet Union.

Too much, however, should not be read into general Soviet policy on non-Russian nationalities from the case of the Crimean Tatars. By any standards their history of forcible deportation and the Soviet Government's subsequent refusal to let them resettle their original home-

lands was exceptional. For the rest the centralised control imposed by the Soviet regime on non-Russian peoples has had mixed effects. The denial of self-determination has been balanced by considerable advances in social welfare, literacy, and economic development. In some non-Russian areas, particularly in central Asia and Siberia, economic progress has been faster than in the rural parts of metropolitan Russia. Even in the Baltic states, where the loss of political independence is still most keenly felt, the standard of living is higher than in the Russian Federation. The colonial stereotype of an imperial power living off the wealth of its dependencies requires considerable modification.

In the first years of his power Khruschev gave some extra concessions to the various nationalities. Non-Russians were promoted in greater numbers to senior posts. But as the split with China developed and in the wake of the Hungarian uprising, a more conservative policy re-emerged, under which the country's nationalities are supposed to 'draw together' and eventually 'merge' into a universal Soviet cultural identity. This policy has been modified by contradictions. At the same time national individuality was reinforced with extra concessions for the use of local languages and some decentralisation of power from Moscow. The formula 'national in form, socialist in content' was devised to cover what is essentially a contradictory policy. Provided a community has a national homeland, the pressures of assimilation are much weaker. The issue of Jewish emigration arose after 1967 partly because Soviet Jews have no homeland and thus less chance to resist the pressures of assimilation. The so-called Jewish Autonomous Region in Siberia known as Birobidzhan is almost inaccessible and has very few Jews in it.

On 17 March 1968 the representatives of the Crimean Tatars met in Moscow and were addressed by Major-General P. G. Grigorenko. Grigorenko had been a lecturer at the Frunze military academy in Moscow until 1961 when he was dismissed for sending an 'open letter' to Moscow voters protesting against restraints on freedom in the Soviet Union. He was arrested in 1964 and sent to the special psychiatric prison, the Serbsky Institute, for a time. He was rearrested in 1970, and in October 1973 was being held in a hospital near Moscow. Active on behalf of many imprisoned writers, Grigorenko took up the case of the Tatars.

K

37 **P. G. Grigorenko**
ON TATAR RIGHTS

. . . It will soon be a quarter of a century since your people were
expelled from their homes and driven from the land of their
ancestors into reservations where living conditions were such
as to presage the inevitable destruction of the entire Crimean
Tatar nation. Yet, to spite their enemies, this hardy, work-
loving people overcame all and survived. After losing forty-six
per cent of their number, they gradually began to regain strength
and resumed the struggle for their national and human rights.

This struggle has resulted in some gains. The system of
forcible resettlement and exile has been ended, and the political
rehabilitation of the Crimean Tatar people has been effected.
This latter step however was taken with various reservations
that did a great deal to detract from the act itself. Most important, the great mass of the Soviet people who had been widely
informed at one time that the Crimean Tatars had sold out the
Crimea was never told that this 'sell-out' was nothing but a
figment of the imagination. But the worst irony was yet to
emerge—namely, the fact that the very edict which effected
the political rehabilitation of the Crimean Tatars simultaneously
legalised the liquidation of that nation. For now, you see, there
are no Crimean Tatars, only 'Tatars who at one time lived in
the Crimea'. . . .

What basis is there for placing your people in a position of
such inequality? Article 123 of the USSR Constitution reads:
'Any direct or indirect restriction of the rights . . . of citizens
on account of their race or nationality is punishable by law.'

Thus the law is on your side. But despite this your rights are
being violated. Why? We think the main reason lies in the fact
that you underestimate your enemy. You think that you arc
dealing only with honest people. This is not so. What happened
to your nation was not the work of Stalin alone. And his
accomplices not only are still alive but hold responsible positions. They are afraid that if you are given back what was

unlawfully taken from you, they may in time be called upon to answer for their participation in such arbitrary rule. Therefore they are doing everything possible to prevent you succeeding in your struggle. After all, if everything is kept as it is, then it gives the impression that there was no lawlessness in the past.

You have chosen tactics that help them to preserve this state of affairs. You address yourselves to the leadership of the party with meekly written pleas which pass through the hands of those who are against your struggle for national equality. And since your pleas concern matters for which there are no indisputable hard and fast rules they are presented to persons who are bound to declare them doubtful, debatable issues, and thus your case becomes enmeshed in judgements and opinions that have nothing to do with the basic problem.

For instance one hears such arguments as 'There is no room in the Crimea for settling the Tatars'; 'if the Tatars move, there will be no-one left in Central Asia to do the work'; . . . 'it would cost a lost of money to resettle them'. And so on . . .

As long as you request, your case is not moving forward, or it is even moving backwards. In order to put a stop to this abnormal situation, you must learn that what is prescribed by law should not be requested; it should be demanded. Start to demand! And demand not bits and pieces, but everything that was unlawfully taken away from you—the re-establishment of a Crimean Autonomous Soviet Socialist Republic.

Do not limit your activity to the writing of petitions. Strengthen your demands by all means available to you under the Constitution. Make good use of the freedom of speech and of the press, of meetings, street processions and demonstrations.

A newspaper is put out for you in Tashkent, but the persons who put it out do not support your movement. Take the newspaper away from them. Elect your own editorial board. If they prevent you from doing this boycott their newspaper and start another of your own. A movement cannot develop normally without its own press.

In your fight don't lock yourselves into a narrow nationalist shell. Form contacts with all progressive people of other nationalities in the Soviet Union, first of all those nationalities among whom you live—Russians, Ukrainians, the nationalities that have been and continue to be subjected to the same indignities as your people.

Don't consider your case to be concerned narrowly with the Government. Seek help from the whole of progressive society and from international organisations. There is a specific name for what was done to your people in 1944. It is genocide, pure and simple . . . If you cannot obtain a solution of the problem within the country, you have a right to appeal to the United Nations and the international tribunal.

Stop begging! Take back that which was taken from you unlawfully. And remember you must not allow your opponents in this just and noble struggle to snatch with impunity the fighters who stand in the front line of your movement.

There have already been a series of trials in Central Asia in which fighters for equal rights for the Crimean Tatars have been sentenced unlawfully and on false grounds. Right now in Tashkent a trial of a similar nature is being prepared for Mamed Enver, Yuri and Savri Osmanov, and others. Do not allow judicial reprisals to be carried out against these people. Demand and obtain for them an open trial, come to it in great numbers, and do not let the court be filled up with specially selected spectators.

SOURCE: *In Quest of Justice*, edited by Abraham Brumberg (Pall Mall Press, 1970)

POLAND 1968

Poland was the first country to react tumultuously to the apparent end to de-Stalinisation which the trial of Sinyavsky and Daniel seemed to embody. Poland's own wave of reform had begun early, in 1956, and been aborted early too, barely 2 years later. The attempt at economic reform, at decentralisation, and at workers' councils had been watered down and reduced to insignificance.

Ten years later a new generation of students, who were mostly too young in 1956, were keen to start out on the road to political change. Some of them were influenced by two young lecturers at Warsaw university, Jacek Kuron and Karol Modzelewski. In 1964 these two distributed a brief manuscript in which they criticised the regime from the left as a 'political bureaucracy' where workers had no real power. They were detained briefly in November and then rewrote their ideas in an 'Open Letter to Fellow Members of the Party'. Rearrested, they were given prison sentences of 3 years each.

The letter, which circulated widely among students and intellectuals, called for the re-establishment of workers' councils and a programme of political strikes designed to undermine the bureaucratic system. It began by arguing that the end of private capitalism had not brought working-class power in Poland.

38 Jacek Kuron and Karol Modzelewski
THE RULE OF THE BUREAUCRACY

According to official doctrine, we live in a socialist country. This thesis is based on the identification of state ownership of the means of production with social ownership. The act of nationalisation transferred industry, transport, and banking into social property, and production relations based on social property are allegedly socialist.

This reasoning is Marxist in appearance. In reality an element fundamentally alien to Marxist theory has been introduced: the formal, legal meaning of ownership. State ownership can conceal various class meanings, depending on the class character of the state. The public sector in the economies of contemporary capitalist countries has nothing in common with social ownership. This is true not only because there exist, beside it, private capitalist corporations, but because the worker in a capitalist state factory is totally deprived of ownership, since he has no real influence in the state and hence no control over his own labour and its product . . .

State ownership of the means of production is only a form of ownership. It is exercised by those social groups to which the state belongs. In a nationalised economic system, only those who participate in, or can influence decisions of an economic nature (such as the use of the means of production and the distribution of and way of profiting from the product) can affect the decisions of the state. Political power is connected with power over the process of production and the distribution of the product.

To whom does power belong in our state? To one monopolistic party—the Polish United Workers' Party (PUWP). All essential decisions are made first in the party, and only later in the offices of the official state power; no important decisions can be made and carried out without the approval of the party authorities. This is called the leading role of the party, and since the monopolistic party considers itself the representative of the interests of the working class, its power is supposed to be a guarantee of working class power . . .

The ruling party is monopolistic. It is impossible for the working class to organise in other parties, and through them to formulate, propagate, and struggle for the realisation of other programmes, other variants of dividing the national product, political concepts other than those of the PUWP. The prohibition by the ruling party against organising the working class is guarded by the entire state apparatus of power and force; the administration, political police, public prosecutor's office, the courts, and also the political organisations led by the party, which unmask and nip in the bud all attempts to undermine the leading role of the PUWP.

But more than a million party members are ordinary citizens; among them, several hundred thousand are workers. What are their chances of influencing the decisions of party and state authorities? The party is not only monopolistic but organised along monolithic lines. All factions, groups with different platforms, organised political currents, are forbidden within the party. Every rank and file member is entitled to his opinion, but he has no right to organise others who think as he does to follow his programme, and he has no right to organise a propaganda and electoral struggle for the realisation of that programme.

Elections to party offices, to conferences and congresses become fictitious under such conditions, since they do not take place on the basis of different programmes and platforms (i.e. an assortment of political alternatives). To exercise political initiative in society you need organisation, but in any attempt to exert influence on the decisions of the 'top', the mass of rank-and-file party members is deprived of organisation, and is atomised and so powerless. The only source of political initiative can be—in the nature of things—organised bodies, i.e. the party apparatus. Like every apparatus it is organised hierarchically; information flows upward, while decisions and orders are handed down from above. As in every hierarchy, the fountainhead of orders is the elite, the group of people who occupy conspicuous position in the hierarchy and who collectively make basic decisions.

In our system the party elite is at one and the same time also the power elite; all decisions relating to state power are made by it and in any case at the top of the party and state hierarchies there exists as a rule a fusion of responsible posts . . .

SOURCE: 'An Open Letter to the Party', by Jacek Kuron & Karol Modzelewski, published in English by *International Socialism* (London 1968)

While the ideas put forward by Kuron and Modzelewski produced a certain echo among intellectuals, more orthodox economists within the party were pressing for Poland to follow the lead being set in the Soviet Union, Hungary, and Czechoslovakia.

Gomulka was unsympathetic. He had run out of ideas. A power struggle began to emerge between two wings of the Polish party. One was represented by Edward Gierek, the Silesian leader, who was in favour of economic modernisation and a more 'technocratic' approach to social and political management. The other was represented by General

Mieczyslaw Moczar, the Minister of the Interior and head of the secret police. They both wanted to see an end to Gomulka's sclerotic leadership. Each hoped for the succession.

They saw their chance in the spring of 1968. A performance of the play Dziady *by Adam Mickiewicz, the great nineteenth-century romantic writer, had been taken off the Warsaw stage after part of the crowd applauded various anti-Russian lines. A number of students protested at the ban and two of them, who happened to be Jews, were expelled from Warsaw University. On 8 March several thousand students demonstrated against the expulsions. Without warning or provocation, the peaceful meeting was set upon and broken up by several busloads of reserve militiamen, so-called party activists.*

As could have been predicted, and probably was, the militiamen's violence led to days of riots and solidarity demonstrations in Warsaw, and at every provincial university. Hundreds of people were arrested.

For the students the episode provided an outlet for suppressed anger and disappointment. Their slogans were not anti-Communist or even anti-Soviet. They demanded political rights, intellectual freedom, strict observance of the Polish constitution, and the release of their arrested colleagues.

The mass media fastened on to the fact that several of the student leaders were Jews. Because many of them were sons and daughters of senior people in the regime (Modzelewski's father had been Foreign Minister), the finger was now pointed at their parents for having brought up subversive children.

Groups within the party launched a campaign against all the so-called 'Zionists' in leading positions. It was claimed that the previous summer during the Six Day War in the Middle East these people had given their sympathies to Israel and opposed Polish support for the Arabs.

On 19 March Wladyslaw Gomulka spoke to 3,000 activists in Warsaw. The speech was carried on national television and radio. Although it was relatively moderate in tone and he was frequently egged on by shouts from the crowd, Gomulka nevertheless laid down that some Jews should be ousted from their jobs.

39 Wladyslaw Gomulka
ON THE JEWS

In the events which have taken place, an active part was played by a section of academic youth of either Jewish origin or nationality (Shouts and applause). I must ask comrades to keep quiet and listen carefully. You can consider it later. (Shouting for about two minutes.) The parents of many of these students occupy more or less responsible positions and also very high posts in our state. It was this circumstance above all which caused the appearance on the crest of these events of the sometimes misunderstood slogan of the struggle against Zionism.

Are there in Poland Jewish nationalists? Are there any supporters of the Zionist ideology? (Shouts of yes, yes.) Comrades, it would be a misunderstanding if anyone should see in Zionism a danger to socialism in Poland, to its present social-political system . . .

But this does not mean, however, that no such problem exists in Poland, which I would call the defining of their own position by some Jews who are Polish citizens. What I mean I will show you by examples. Last year, during the Israeli aggression against the Arab states, a definite number of Jews displayed their willingness, in various forms, to go to Israel to take part in the war against the Arabs. It is beyond doubt that this category of Jews—Polish citizens—is linked intellectually and emotionally not with Poland but with Israel. They were certainly Jewish nationalists regardless of their nationality. I suppose that this category of Jews will leave Poland sooner or later (Loud and prolonged cheers).

We have in the past opened our frontiers wide to all those who did not want to be citizens of our country and who decided to leave for Israel. We are also prepared to issue emigration passports to those who consider Israel their fatherland (Loud applause) . . .

It is beyond doubt that today there are also in Poland a certain number of people, Polish citizens, who do not consider themselves to be either Poles or Jews. One should not blame them for this. No-one can impose the feeling of nationality on anyone else. But because of their cosmopolitan feelings, such people should avoid any employment in which the affirmation of one's nationality is essential (Applause).

Finally there is the third, most numerous group of our citizens of Jewish origin, who have grown roots in the soil on which they were born and to whom Poland is the only father-land (Applause) in which they occupy responsible state and party positions, and work in leading positions in various spheres of our life. Through their work and struggle many of them have honestly served People's Poland and the cause of socialism, and the party greatly appreciates this (Applause). But no matter what the feelings of Polish citizens of Jewish origin are, our party opposes with full determination all symptoms of anti-semitism . . .

Factory workers, the working class, though full of justified indignation towards the reactionary instigators and organisers of street brawls, should at the same time reject all uninformed rumours which derive either from fantasy or from gossip or from the enemy's diversionary activities. Let us remember that throwing mud at innocent people belongs to the arsenal of methods used by the reaction in its fight against our party, our system. Before any kind of allegation against anybody is raised publicly, it must be previously checked in the appropriate party documents. We shall not spare the guilty. We shall defend the innocent.

SOURCE: Translation by Monitoring Service of the BBC, and reprinted by permission of the BBC

Gomulka's line did not satisfy Moczar and his supporters. The old wartime split in the party reappeared. The 'partisans' who had spent the war underground in Poland fighting a guerrilla campaign against the Nazis had always felt some reserve towards the 'Muscovites' who had had a relatively sheltered war. Many of them were Jews.

After the war Stalin trusted them more than the partisans, whom he suspected of having anti-Russian feelings. The Moczar forces now began a vicious witchhunt against many of the 'Muscovites' on the grounds that they were 'Zionists' and unpatriotic. Thousands of the last 30,000 Jews left in Poland were dismissed or emigrated.

In June 1968 the Warsaw literary journal Miesiecznik Literacki *published an article by Andrzej Werblan, a central committee member. Under the title 'A Contribution to the Genesis of the Conflict' he attempted to give a coherent analysis to the campaign. The article brought all the old bitterness to the surface and concluded on an anti-semitic note that 'the irregular ethnic composition' in Poland's central institutions should be 'corrected'.*

40 Andrzej Werblan
WHY ARE THERE SO MANY JEWS?

. . . Why is it that a relatively large number of people of Jewish origin can be found among certain groups of the intelligentsia in our country? Their number is not so large as is generally believed but all the same it is much larger than one might expect on the basis of the percentage of Jews in our society. Why can we spot a particular susceptibility to revisionism and the development of Jewish nationalism in general and Zionism in particular in the attitudes of certain Jewish milieux or people of Jewish origin? . . .

We must go back not only to the years of 1956–57 but still further to the inter-war period and particularly to the occupation and the first years after the liberation . . .

A considerable part of the Jewish population in pre-war Poland was represented by the poor—cottage industry workers, stall owners, craftsmen, and small factory workers who lived in misery. It is quite understandable that these milieux gravitated towards the political movement of the left.

The Communist Party of Poland consistently opposed any discrimination against national minorities. This fact also favoured the growth of its influence among national minorities including the Jewish population and even among part of the youth from well-to-do milieux of the Jewish middle class . . .

Under the conditions of the Nazi occupation, pre-war party workers of Jewish stock with only a few exceptions were unable to share in political work in occupied Poland. Most of this section of the former KPP activists found themselves in emigration in the USSR, and together with numerous Poles, KPP members, leftwing socialists and populists shared actively in the creation of the Union of Polish Patriots (ZPP) and the 1st Army of the Polish Armed Forces. Hence the relatively high proportion of activists of Jewish ancestry . . .

Objective circumstances meant that these activists, living in emigration, did not undergo the renewing and refreshing ideological therapy of underground work in the occupied country, in which new party cadres grew and became politically educated, in which the party's bonds with the masses were in the process of being established . . .

They were marked by a peculiar sense of superiority with regard to the fighters at home. On their return to the country they felt called upon to define the political line of the people's state . . . After the Twentieth Congress of the Communist Party of the Soviet Union important cadre changes were made. A part of the party cadres was burdened with actual responsibility for serious dogmatic errors, sectarianism and infringement of lawabidingness. Politically justified criticism was directed against them, and these people had to depart from posts of responsibility or move over to a side track . . . As regards activists of Jewish origin, they often branded all ostracism against themselves as anti-semitism. As a result regressive political processes appeared in the course of the last ten years among these activists and party members of Jewish origin. They composed a milieu afflicted with political frustration, alienation, and bitterness. An atmosphere favourable for the spread of revisionism and opposition towards the party was born, nationalist group solidarity and Zionism was consolidated, and cases of open treason took place . . .

A specially bad political atmosphere was created in the institutions where there was a concentration of people of Jewish origin. These institutions—there were not too many of them after all—included, for instance, publishing houses where comrades recalled from other high posts were employed, or some colleges where special regulations on service and the place's specific character made it difficult to change the cadre which had been constituted years ago . . .

Of course it should always be borne in mind that revisionism has remained the party's chief ideological danger. Jewish nationalism in general and Zionism as its specific extreme have done considerable harm but as a political manifestation they can only act on a limited scale and their life cannot be long. In Poland the potential for these trends is small. The correction of the irregular ethnic composition in the central institutions where it is necessary will go a long way towards removing this problem from the agenda.

SOURCE: *Miesiecznik Literacki* (June 1968), translated in *The Anti-Jewish Campaign in Present-day Poland*, published by the Institute of Jewish Affairs (1968)

Gomulka began to see that the campaign was getting out of his control. The fact that his wife was Jewish put him in an awkward position. He understood very well that he himself was coming under attack. It was widely expected that at the fifth congress of the Polish party in November his rivals would unseat him.

In the event the Czechoslovak crisis saved him. After the invasion, in which Poland loyally took part, stability became the watchword of the hour. The Soviet leadership did not want any changes elsewhere and their backing enabled Gomulka to remain after all in power for a little longer.

CZECHOSLOVAKIA 1968

Unlike Poland or Hungary Czechoslovakia went through no real de-Stalinisation after 1953. Political, intellectual, and cultural life remained in a frozen state while at the top, in the tradition of Stalin himself, the two main positions, the presidency and the first secretaryship of the party, were in the hands of one man, Antonin Novotny.

This anomaly survived in the country which had had the largest Communist party after the war and where democratic traditions were stronger than anywhere else in Eastern Europe. The anachronism could not last, and underneath the ice on the surface of public life a current of reform began to gather force. Even more than in the other countries, it was a socialist current. Hardly anyone wanted a return to capitalism. The aim was to try to blend a democratic and open political system on to a socialist economic order.

The first stirrings were felt in 1962 soon after the Twenty-second Congress of the Soviet party. Novotny succumbed to pressures and agreed to set up a committee to review the political trials of the 1950s. The old Stalinist leader of the Slovak party, Karol Bacilek, was replaced in 1963 by a moderate, Alexander Dubcek. Reformist writers, film-makers and playwrights began to touch in a restrained way on the 'cult of the personality' and other Stalinist deformations. By 1966 the economists had persuaded Novotny to accept a reform of the planning system (see Document 34).

At the beginning of 1967 Novotny took fright and tried to block the reforms. Several of the more outspoken editors and commentators were removed from their posts. Some avant-garde films were suppressed. At the writers' congress later in the year a number of bolder authors decided to challenge the mood of reaction openly. They called for a relaxation of censorship and an honest appraisal of Czechoslovakia's problems.

In Slovakia a powerful movement within the party was also preparing to challenge Novotny's Czech-dominated policies which, they claimed, denied Slovakia an adequate voice in the country's affairs. In January 1968 a disparate coalition in the central committee removed Novotny as First Secretary and replaced him with Alexander Dubcek.

His election unleashed a torrent of suggestions and pressures for radical reform in the political sphere. The main line was that the leadership of the Communist Party had abused its position too much in the recent past by stifling debate. It was essential to find institutional ways for the different interests in society to make their voices heard without of course going back to a Western parliamentary system.

In February 1968 Gustav Husak wrote a critical article in the weekly journal of the Slovak Writers' Union. He attacked the self-congratulatory tone of party discussions in the past. Husak had been a leading figure in the partisan movement in Slovakia and in the immediate postwar period. In 1954 he was sentenced as a 'bourgeois nationalist' to life imprisonment. Nine years later he was released and rehabilitated. After the invasion in August 1968 he became the spokesman of the 'realists' and in April 1969 replaced Dubcek as First Secretary of the Czechoslovak Communist Party.

41 Gustav Husak
PROPAGANDA AND ANALYSIS ARE NOT
THE SAME

. . . I believe that once again we have to learn a very simple thing: to reflect, write, and speak soberly and critically about public affairs. We used to know this, but somehow we seem to have 'forgotten' it in the course of time. We were full of festive pathos, jubilant about our victories and successes, and carried away by revolutionary, or also pseudo-revolutionary romanticism and utopianism. Propaganda and critical analysis are not the same thing.

A style of speaking about public questions, a vocabulary and jargon was adopted which resembled the canons of old Christian prayerbooks: a whole ritual regulating who was allowed to say what about whom and what to think. And this was our guidance, supposed to enable us to know everything, understand everything and find the correct solution for everything at the right time. Only real life did not follow these rules . . .

A critical current of thought and evaluation has grown up and is still growing in this country, a current of realisation that the road towards the future success and progress in every sphere requires the critical overcoming of the past and present state of affairs; that intoxication with the glory of victories of the past, their exaggeration, the suppression of shortcomings and existing conflicts must lead to a stagnation of thought and action. And stagnation means to lag behind.

I think that we shall have to reflect a great deal about how and why our society got into its present state of affairs, which is not exactly satisfactory in a number of far from insignificant spheres (whether of a political, economic, ethnic or other kind). I think that a more modest appreciation will emerge from a critical analysis than that which has hailed 'the victorious road from February', leading from victory to victory, from success to success, for so many years—as if we were a world miracle which, aside from the imperialistic reactionaries and their agents, knew no other obstacles or could clear hurdles with the elegance of a race horse, as if sacred beings, foreordained to be inscribed in the lists of socialist saints, were our leaders and not normal people with good and bad qualities whose work must be checked and controlled.

This fetishism too served as opium, obscuring the critical approach towards problems and people. Only a fool would want to give up any of the assets which our nations have created over the course of the years; and each of us could make up a long list of those assets . . .

The stream of revival in our party and society has grown in strength in the past few years and has swept through the conservative forces to a position whence it wants to and can become the decisive factor in the determination of our present and future socialist development. The settlement of the problems which have accumulated and the planning of the modernisation of our society require a critical analysis of the ground we have traversed to date, a critical analysis of individual problems, methods, and people. Marx's critical method—'de omnibus est dubitandum' (everything must be open to question—Trans)— must apply in particular at times of great change of this kind. And at the same time we must also heed Lenin's reminder that fundamental problems of society must be brought out into the open and solved before the eyes of the broad working masses, with their co-operation and support, and with their full commitment.

Periods of revolution have done away with secret diplomacy and stage settings. This also is a sign of a progressive trend and a guarantee of victory . . .

SOURCE: Husak. 'Notes on the February Events', first published in *Kulturny Zivot* (2 February 1968)

The various currents for reform came together at the plenary meeting of the central committee in April. The party adopted a 24,000 word 'Action Programme', entitled 'Czechoslovakia's Road to Socialism', setting out its plans for reform. Although the programme was inevitably a compromise which did not go as far as some of the more outspoken intellectuals would have liked, it was a considerable advance over the pre-1968 position.

The programme gave assurances that freedom of assembly would be implemented 'this year' and that censorship would be eliminated. Victims of the purges would be rehabilitated more quickly, and more exact and precise guarantees would protect the right to hold minority opinions. The constitution would guarantee the right to travel, and Czechoslovak citizens would even have the right to live abroad for extended periods. The programme promised to limit the activity of the security police simply to matters involving state security.

Its central section dealt with the deformations of democracy in the past and the role of the party in the future. The party had to earn its respect. It could not impose it. As for reconciling different interest groups, this job was given to the revived National Front, which was supposed to become a forum for genuinely thrashing out political differences.

42 Czechoslovak Communist Party
ACTION PROGRAMME

A deeper reason why out-of-date economic methods were maintained was that the political system itself was deformed. Socialist democracy did not expand. The revolutionary dictator-

L

ship deteriorated into bureaucracy and held up progress in every aspect of life in Czechoslovakia. Thus political mistakes were added to economic difficulties . . . A great deal of the efforts, activity, and energy of party and state workers was wasted. And when we add the external political difficulties of the early 1960's, then a serious economic crisis ensued. It is this that has caused the difficulties with which workers are confronted day by day . . . the catastrophic state of housing, the precarious state of the transport system, poor quality goods and public services, the lack of a civilised environment to live in— all factors which tangibly affect the human being and are the vital concern of a socialist society. Bitterness grew among the people and a feeling that in spite of all the successes achieved and effort expended, socialism was making progress with great difficulty, with fatal delays and with many imperfections in the moral and political relationships between people . . .

Socialist democracy did not develop in the party itself . . . criticism was silenced or even suppressed, and mistakes were not corrected. Party bodies took over the tasks of state and economic bodies and social organisations, and this resulted in an incorrect merging of the party and state management, to the monopoly of power in some sectors, to unqualified interference, to the undermining of initiative, and to the growth of a cult of mediocrity and unhealthy anonymity. Irresponsibility and lack of discipline increased . . .

At present it is most important that the party practises such a policy that it fully merits its leading role in society. We believe that at present this is a condition for the socialist development of the country.

The Communist party enjoys the voluntary support of the people; it does not realise its leading role by ruling over society but by serving its free, progressive socialist development in a devoted way. The party cannot impose its authority; this has to be won again and again by party activity. It cannot enforce its line by means of directives but by the work of its members, and the truthfulness of its ideals.

In the past the leading role of the party was often conceived as a monopolistic concentration of power in the hands of party bodies. This corresponded to the false thesis that the party is the instrument of the dictatorship of the proletariat. This harmful conception weakened the initiative and responsibility of the state, economic and social institutions, damaged the party's authority and impeded it in carrying out its real functions. The party's aim is not to become a universal caretaker of our society, to bind every organisation and to regulate every step taken in everyday life with its directives. Its mission lies primarily in arousing socialist initiative, in showing the ways to and actual possibilities of communist perspectives, and in winning over all the workers to them using systematic persuasion, as well as through the personal examples of communists. At the same time the party cannot turn into an organisation which would only influence society through its ideas and its programmes. With its membership and its bodies, it has to develop the functions of a practical organisation and a political force in society . . .

As a representative of the interests of the most progressive part of all the state—thus also a representative of the aims and perspectives of that society—the party cannot represent the whole gamut of social interests. The political expression of the many-sided interests of society is the National Front. Its nature expresses the unity of the social classes, interest groups, and the different nationalities in this society. The policy of the Communist party must not lead to non-Communists getting the impression that their rights and freedom are limited by the role of the party. Far from it: they must see in the party's activity a guarantee of their rights, freedom and interests. We want to achieve, and we shall achieve, a state of affairs in which the party, at its basic organisational level, will have informal, natural authority, based on its ability to work and manage society and on the moral qualities of its functionaries.

Within the framework of the democratic rules of a socialist state, communists must over and over again struggle to engage the voluntary support of the majority for the party line. If party resolutions and directives fail to express correctly the needs and potentialities of the whole of society, they must be altered. The party must try to make sure that its members— as the most active workers in their particular sphere—have a corresponding weight and influence in society, and hold functions in state, economic and social bodies. But this, however, must not lead to the practice of appointing party members to functions without regard to the principle that the leading representatives of institutions of the whole of society are chosen by society itself and by its various components, and that the functionaries of these components are responsible to every citizen and to every member of social organisations. It is necessary to abolish the discriminating practice and creation of a 'cadre ceiling' for people who are not members of the party.

The most important thing is to reform the whole political system to allow for the dynamic development of socialist social relations, combine broad democracy with scientific, highly qualified management, strengthen the social order, stabilise social relations and maintain social discipline. The basic structure of the political system must at the same time provide firm guarantees against a return to the old methods of subjectivism and high-handedness from a position of power . . .

SOURCE: *Rude Pravo* (10 April 1968), translated in *Czechoslovakia* by Andrew Oxley, Alex Pravda and Andrew Ritchie (Allen Lane, the Penguin Press 1973)

During the next few months the heady mood of spring evaporated a little. It was now a question of putting the Action Programme into practice. Within the party conservatives had begun to take fright at the extent of the reform movement, and a struggle was shaping up between them and the progressives. Eyes turned to the forthcoming party congress which would elect a new central committee and decide once and for all which group ruled the party. Czechoslovakia's Warsaw Pact allies were voicing undisguised alarm at the scope and speed of the internal changes.

Inside Czechoslovakia press discussion was totally free. It is no exaggeration to say that in those days the country had the freest press in the world, with censorship abolished and no libel laws as an alternative restraint. On 27 June 1968 four Czech papers published 'an open letter to workers, farmers, officials, artists, scholars, scientists and technicians, and everyone'. Called 'The Two Thousand Words', the letter appealed to everyone to keep close watch to ensure that the reforms promised by the party were really put into action. 'Let us drop the impossible demand that someone from on high should always provide us with a single explanation and a single simple moral . . . In the days to come we must gird ourselves with our own initiative and make our own decisions.' It ended by drawing attention to the threat of foreign intervention and promised that 'we can show our Government that we will stand by it with weapons if need be'. The party leadership felt it had to disown, at least in moderate terms, the outspoken letter, but the mass media reported it and it had wide public support.

43 Ludvík Vaculík
THE TWO THOUSAND WORDS

The first threat to our national life was the war. Then came other evil days, and events menacing to the nation's spiritual wellbeing and character. It was with high hopes that most of the nation welcomed the socialist programme. But its direction fell into the hands of the wrong people. It would not have mattered so much that they lacked adequate experience in the affairs of state, factual knowledge, or philosophical education, if only they had had enough common prudence and decency to listen to the opinion of others and agree to being gradually replaced by more able men.

After enjoying great popular confidence immediately after the war, the Communist Party by degrees bartered this confidence away for office, till it had all the offices and nothing else. We have to say this and it is well known to those of us who are communists and who are as disappointed as the rest at the way things turned out. The leaders' mistaken policies transformed a political party and an alliance based on ideas into an organization for exerting power, one which proved highly attractive to egotists itching to wield authority, to cowards with an eye to the main chance, to people with bad consciences. The influx of members such as these affected the character and behaviour of the Party, whose internal arrangements made it impossible— short of scandalous incidents—for honest members to gain influence and adapt it continuously to modern conditions. Many communists fought against this decline, but they did not manage to prevent what ensued.

Conditions inside the Communist Party served as pattern and cause for identical conditions in the State. The Party's association with the State robbed it of the asset of separation from executive power. No one criticized the activities of the State and of the economic bodies. Parliament forgot how to hold proper debates, the government forgot how to govern properly, and managers how to manage properly. Elections lost their significance, the law carried no weight. We could not trust our representatives on any committee, or if we could, there was no point in asking them for anything because they were powerless. Worse still, we could scarcely trust one another. Personal and collective honour decayed. Honesty was a useless virtue, assessment by merit unheard of. Most people accordingly lost interest in public affairs . . .

We all of us bear responsibility for the present state of affairs. But those of us that are communists bear more than others, and those who acted as component parts, or as instruments of unchecked power bear most of all. It was the power of a self-willed band of men, spreading out through the party apparatus into every district and community. It was this apparatus which decided what might and might not be done, which ran the co-operative farms for the co-operative farmers, ran the factories for the workers, and ran the National Committees for the public. No organizations, not even communist ones, were really controlled by their own members. The chief sin and deception of these rulers was to have represented their own whims as the 'will of the workers.' Were we to accept this pretence, we would have to blame the workers today for the decline of our economy, for crimes committed against the innocent, for the introduction of censorship to prevent anyone writing about these things; the workers would be to blame for misconceived investments, trading losses, and the housing shortage.

Obviously no sensible person will believe the working class responsible for such things. We all know, and every worker knows especially well, that he had virtually no say in deciding anything. Working class functionaries were given their voting instructions by someone else. While many workers imagined they were the rulers, it was an especially trained stratum of Party and State officials who ruled in their name. In effect it was these men who stepped into the shoes of the deposed ruling class and themselves came to constitute the new authority.

Let us in fairness say that some of them long ago realized the bad trick history had played. We can recognize such individuals today by the way they are rectifying old wrongs, making good their blunders, handing back powers of decision to rank-and-file Party members and members of the public, setting limits to the authority and size of the bureaucracy. They share our opposition to backward views among Party members. But a large proportion of officials have been resistant to change and are still influential. They still wield the instruments of power, especially at district and community level, where they can employ them in secret and without fear of prosecution.

Since the start of this year we have been experiencing a regenerative process of democratization. It started inside the Communist Party. We have to say this and it is well known even to those communists amongst us who no longer had hopes of anything good emerging from that quarter. It must also be added, of course, that there was nowhere else where the process could have started. For after 20 years the communists were alone able to conduct some sort of political existence; it was only communist criticism which had any impact on courses of action; it was only the opposition inside the Communist Party which had the privilege of contact with antagonistic views. The effort and initiative now displayed by democratically minded communists, then, is only a partial repayment of the debt owed by the entire Party to the non-communists whom it had been holding down in a position of inequality. No thanks, accordingly, are due to the Communist Party, though perhaps it should be granted, that the Party is making an honest effort at the eleventh hour to save its own honour and the nation's.

The regenerative process introduces nothing particularly new into our life. It revives ideas and topics, many of which are older than the errors of our socialism, while others, having arisen below the surface of visible history, should long ago have found expression but were instead repressed.

Let us not foster the illusion that it is the power of truth which makes such ideas victorious. Their victory has been due rather to the weakness of the old leaders, evidently debilitated in advance, by 20 years of rule with no one standing in their way. All the defects hidden in the foundations and ideology of the system must clearly have reached their full maturity. So let us not overestimate the effect of the writers' and students' criticisms. The source of social changes is the economy. The true word makes its mark only when it is spoken under conditions that have been properly prepared. Properly prepared conditions— in our context, that must unfortunately include the whole impoverishment of our society and the complete collapse of the old system of government, under which certain sorts of politicians calmly and quietly compromised themselves at our expense. Truth, then, is not winning the day; truth is merely what remains when everything else has been frittered away. So there is no reason for national jubilation: simply for fresh hope.

At this moment of hope, albeit hope still threatened, we turn to you. It took several months before many of us believed it was safe to speak up; many of us do not think it safe even yet. But speak up we did, and we exposed ourselves so far that we have no choice but to complete our plan to humanize the regime. If we did not, the old forces would take a cruel revenge.

We turn above all to those who so far have only waited. The time now approaching will decide the issue for years to come.

The time now approaching is the summer holiday time, when our inclination, ingrained by habit, will be to let everything slip. But it is a safe bet that our dear adversaries will give themselves no summer breathing-space; they will rally everyone who is under any obligation to them and take steps, even now, to ensure themselves a quiet Christmas! Let us watch carefully how things develop, let us try to understand them and have our answers ready. Let us drop the impossible demand that someone from on high should always provide us with a single explanation and a single, simple moral. Everyone will have to draw his own conclusions on his own responsibility. Common, agreed conclusions can only be reached in discussion, which requires freedom of speech—the only democratic achievement to our credit this year.

But in the days to come we must gird ourselves with our own initiative and make our own decisions.

To begin with, we shall oppose the view sometimes heard that a democratic revival can be achieved without the communists, or even in opposition to them. This would be unjust, and foolish too. The communists have their organizations ready built, and in these we must support the progressive wing. They have their experienced officials, and they still have in their hands, after all, the crucial levels and press-buttons. On the other hand they have come before the public with their Action Programme. This is a programme for the first evening out of the crassest inequalities, and no one else has a programme in such specific detail. We must demand that they produce local Action Programmes in public in every district and community. Then the issue will suddenly revolve around very ordinary and long-awaited acts of justice . . .

People have recently been worried that the democratization programme has come to a halt. This feeling is partly a sign of fatigue after the excitement of events, but partly it reflects the truth. The season of astonishing revelations, dismissals from high office, and heady speeches couched in language of unaccustomed daring—all this is over. But the struggle between opposing forces has merely become somewhat less open; the fight continues over the content and formulation of the laws, over the scope of practical measures. Besides, we must give the new people time for their work, the new ministers, prosecutors, chairmen, and secretaries. They are entitled to time in which to prove themselves fit or unfit . . .

The everyday quality of our future democracy depends on what happens in the factories, and on what happens to the factories. Despite all our discussions, it is the economic managers who have us in their grasp. Good managers must be sought out and promoted. True, we are all badly paid in comparison with people in the developed countries, some of us worse than others. We can ask for more money; money can be printed and so devalued. Let us rather ask the directors and the chairmen of boards to tell us what they want to produce and at what cost, who they want to sell it to and at what price, what profit will be made, and of that, how much will be reinvested in modernizing production and how much left over for distribution.

Under dreary-looking headlines a hard battle is being reflected in the press—the battle of democracy versus soft jobs. The workers . . . can intervene in this battle by electing the right people to managements and works councils. And . . . they can help themselves best by electing as their trade union representatives natural leaders, able and honourable men without regard to party affiliation.

Though one cannot at present expect more of the central political bodies, it is urgent to achieve more at district and community level. Let us demand the departure of people who abused their power, damaged public property, acted dishonourably or brutally. Ways must be found of bringing them to resign. To mention a few: public criticism, resolutions, demonstrations, collections to buy presents for them on their retirement, strikes and picketing at their front doors. But we should reject any illegal, indecent or boorish methods, which they would exploit to bring influence to bear on Alexander Dubcek . . .

The summer traffic throughout the Republic will enhance interest in the settlement of constitutional relations between Czechs and Slovaks. Let us consider federalization as a method of solving the question of nationalities, and otherwise merely as one of several important measures designed to democratize the system. In itself this particular measure may not necessarily give even the Slovaks a better life. The problem of government is not solved by having separate governments in the Czech lands and in Slovakia. Rule by a State and Party bureaucracy could still go on: in Slovakia indeed it might be strengthened by the claim that it had 'won more freedom.'

There has been great alarm recently over the prospect of foreign forces intervening in our development. Whatever superior forces may face us, all we can do is to stick to our own positions, behave decently, and start nothing ourselves. We can show our Government that we will stand by it, with weapons if need be, if it will do what we give it a mandate to do. And we can assure our allies that we shall observe our treaties of alliance, friendship and trade. Irritable reproaches and ill-argued suspicions on our part can only make things harder for our Government, and bring no benefit to ourselves. In any case, the only way we can achieve relations of equality is to improve our domestic situation and carry the regenerative process so far as to elect one day statesmen with enough courage, honour and political sagacity to create such relations and keep them so. But this is a problem that faces all governments of small countries everywhere.

This spring a great opportunity came to us again, as it came after the end of the war. Again we have the chance to take into our own hands our common cause—which for working purposes we call socialism—and give it a form more appropriate to our once good reputation, and to that fairly good opinion we originally had of ourselves. The spring is over and will never return. By winter we shall know all.

SOURCE: 'The Two Thousand Words' by Ludvik Vaculik, published on 27 June 1968 by *Literarni Listy, Prace, Mlada Fronta*, and *Zemedelske Noviny*

The conclusion of 'The Two Thousand Words' that 'by winter we shall know all' was prophetic. The document was severely attacked in the Soviet press. Two and a half weeks later, at a meeting in Warsaw which the Czechoslovak leaders declined to attend, the party leaders of the USSR, Bulgaria, the German Democratic Republic, Hungary and Poland wrote a stern letter to the Czechs.

Although they disclaimed any wish to intervene in the internal affairs of another party, they went on: 'At the same time we cannot agree to have hostile forces push your country away from the road of socialism and create a danger of Czechoslovakia being severed from the socialist community. This is something more than your concern. It is the common concern of all the Communist and Workers' Parties and States.'

The letter concluded more menacingly still that by 'capitalising on the weakening of the party leadership of the country and demagogically abusing the slogan of "democratisation" the forces of reaction have triggered off a campaign against the Communist Party of Czechoslovakia, clearly seeking to abolish the party's leading role, to subvert the socialist system, and to place Czechoslovakia in opposition to the other socialist countries . . .'

The Czechoslovak answer came a few days later in a television speech to the nation by Alexander Dubcek. He replied to the strong language of the Warsaw letter in indirect terms, saying that the fate of socialism was in good hands 'for it is in the hands of our people'. He also reassured the Czechs and Slovaks that no part of the Action Programme would be given up.

44 Alexander Dubcek
ADDRESS TO THE NATION

. . . We have paid dearly for the practice of the past years. This is why the leaders of the party put such emphasis on the possibility of citizens applying their creativity and satisfying their wishes and needs, so that our country may not lag behind economically and culturally, and chiefly that in the service of the people a policy may be followed that means socialism does not lose its human face.

After many years an atmosphere has been created in our country in which everyone can publicly and without fear, openly and with dignity, express his opinion and thus test the fact that the cause of this country and the cause of socialism is the cause of all of us. By an open and honest policy, by a sincere and thorough elimination of the residue of past years, our Party is gradually regaining its badly shaken confidence.

Therefore we say openly, calmly but determinedly, that we realise what is now at stake: there is no other path than for the people of this country to achieve profound, democratic, and socialist changes in our life. We do not want to give up in the least any of the principles we expressed in the Action Programme and which were again repeated in the stand taken by the Presidium. The Communist Party relies on the voluntary support of the people; we do not carry out our guiding role by ruling over society, but by serving their free, progressive and socialist development in the most dedicated way. We cannot assert our authority by giving orders, but by the work of our members, and by the justice of our ideals.

Since in the preceding period the masses, our people, were not satisfied with the way our policy was carried out in this country, since they were not satisfied with the practices used in carrying out Party policy, then it is natural that if the Party wants to carry out its policy, it cannot change the masses of the people, but we must change the leadership. And this leadership must change its political methods to correspond truly to the interests and desires of our nations, of our Czechoslovak homeland, of our Republic.

Developing socialism in a free society, on the basis of Marxism-Leninism, modern in its orientation and profoundly humane, is the great patriotic task and at the same time our truly international obligation towards the worldwide workers and communist movement.

Our people's land is like a wedge inserted among the socialist countries and we shall protect this strategic position of socialism like the apple of our eye. We have not been untrue to our friends and allies, we have loyally carried out our pledges and shall continue to do so, the pledges to defend the camp of the Warsaw Pact.

We consider that the necessary basis for our independence in a tempestuous world, in Europe and throughout the world, is the alliance with the socialist countries, especially with the Soviet Union, with which we are united by profound, emotionally rooted and sincere friendship. We are demonstrating actively our unswerving loyalty to proletarian internationalism. It is loyalty to these principles that compels us not to yield an inch in the path that we entered after the January plenary session of the central committee. The revolutionary movement can be strong only if every individual link in the movement is strong.

The fate of socialism in our country is in good hands for it is in the hands of our workers and farmers, and our working intelligentsia to whom the cause of socialism has become their own. No-one can doubt the maturity and responsibility of this people. Long years of struggle for national existence and then for the statehood of Czechoslovakia here at the crossroads of European history has armed our people with perseverance and experiences which were not broken by any previous oppression. Our nations have a sense of justice, freedom and humanity. They are determined to defend everything which is good that they have accomplished and are loyal to their friends.

In the entire period of existence of our party we have never given any reason to doubt our loyalty to internationalism, to communist ideals, and the international workers' and communist movement. It would be an illusion to suppose that our party and people could go through this complicated period of difficulties and obstacles without making any mistake or having no shortcomings whatever. We are faced with deciding fateful questions and problems which have been accumulating in the party and in our society over the past years. The May plenary session of the central committee, and other measures taken by the party show that we are gradually solving and overcoming these problems, in the party as a whole and under the control of the people.

Therefore the leadership of our party, its democratically elected bodies, the membership of the party and the public and its representatives are becoming convinced that a real turn for the better is taking place in our country and that socialism is taking on a form that is near and dear to everyone, and that it is becoming stronger and putting down new, deep roots. This is decisive for any judgement on the real situation in Czechoslovakia and on the progress of our party in building socialism. Who else and who better can comprehend and understand the interests, desires, and needs of our working people than this party which works in this country, is linked with its working people, who better than the Government which was elected by the will of the people and than the representatives of our people in other elected bodies?

SOURCE: Dubcek's television speech (18 July 1968); English translation by the Svoboda Publishing House, Prague, and reprinted in *Czechoslovakia 1968*, by Philip Windsor and Adam Roberts (1969)

Unconvinced, the Soviet leaders summoned the entire Czechoslovak presidium to a meeting. Held at Cierna-nad-Tisou on the frontier between the two countries it seemed to provide a breathing space. The Czechs came back thinking they had convinced the Soviet leaders that the reforms were no threat to Communism.

Three weeks later on the night of 20 August Soviet transport planes landed in Prague and tanks rolled out. The Czechoslovak presidium, meeting during the night, immediately condemned the invasion as a violation of sovereignty.

The invasion was greeted by a shocked and disbelieving public. In the streets people argued in Russian with equally bewildered tank drivers. Clandestine radio stations broadcast appeals to the troops to go home. Many of the appeals came from workers meeting in their factories. A typical one was issued 'in the name of all the workers of the national enterprise Polygrafia in Prague's District Twelve'.

45 APPEAL AGAINST THE INVASION

Comrades!

You came to us convinced that you were defending the cause of socialism in our country. You yourselves have seen that there is peace here and that no counter-revolutionary elements are active. The Communist Party of Czechoslovakia continues to lead the people on the basis of socialism and Marxist-Leninist teaching. That is why we see no reason for the occupation of our territory by allied armies of the Warsaw Pact. After our own sad experiences with German militarism, we are capable of defending our Western frontier in the knowledge that we are defending it not only for our sake but for the entire socialist peace camp, of which we are a party. We therefore do not view your arrival as we did in 1945 when you came to liberate us from Hitler's oppression; we view it as an unwanted occupation. This armed strike against the sovereignty of our state will disturb our mutual friendly relations for a long time to come. We ask therefore: leave our territory as friends and do not interfere with our internal development. A further step-up in your activity here will create a tragic misunderstanding.

SOURCE: *The Czech Black Book*, prepared by the Institute of History of the Czechoslovak Academy of Sciences, edited by Robert Littell, and published by Praeger Publishers, Inc, New York and Pall Mall Press, London

46 Student
AN APPEAL TO ALL STUDENTS OF THE WORLD

I am a Czech student, twenty-two years old. As I am writing this proclamation, Soviet tanks are stationed in a large park under my windows. The barrels of their guns are trained on a Government building decorated with a huge sign 'For socialism and peace'. I remember hearing this slogan ever since I was able to grasp the meaning of objects around me. But only during the last seven months has this slogan slowly acquired its original meaning. For seven months, my country has been led by people who wanted to prove, probably for the first time in the history of mankind, that socialism and democracy can exist side by side. Nobody knows where these people are now. I don't know whether I shall ever see or hear them again. There is much that I don't know. For example, how long will it take the Soviet troops to silence free radio stations, which are telling the nation the truth? I don't know either whether I shall be able to finish my university studies or meet my friends from abroad again. I could carry on and on like this, but somehow everything seems to be losing its original value. At three o'clock in the morning of 21 August 1968 I have opened my eyes on a world entirely different from that in which only six hours before I had gone to sleep.

You will think, perhaps, that the Czech people have behaved like cowards because they did not fight. But you cannot stand up to tanks with bare hands. I want to assure you that Czechs and Slovaks have acted as a politically mature nation, which may be broken physically but not morally. This is why I write. The only way you can help is: don't forget Czechoslovakia. Please help our passive resistance by increasing the pressure of public opinion around the world. Think of Czechoslovakia even when this country ceases to be sensational news.

SOURCE: *Student*, undated first special edition (probably 23 August 1968), reprinted in *The Czech Black Book*, op cit

M

Soviet motives for invading were many and varied. It is impossible to say which one had priority. They were afraid of several possibilities. As in Hungary in 1956 Czechoslovakia might turn neutral and leave the Warsaw Pact. The various internal reforms might 'contaminate' the rest of the Soviet camp. The experiment giving Slovakia a meaningful role in the Czechoslovak federation might arouse dangerously similar thoughts in the nearby Ukraine (one of the key Soviet leaders at the Warsaw meeting was Pyotr Shelest, the Ukrainian party secretary). The revival of workers' councils could reawaken similar ideas in Poland. The liberalisation of the mass media was a threat to all the regimes.

Whatever its motives, the Soviet Union tried urgently to justify its actions in international law. The invasion caused particular confusion among the Western communist parties, nearly all of whom condemned it. So did Yugoslavia and Rumania.

On 28 September Pravda *published a theoretical commentary explaining the limitations of national sovereignty under socialism. Western commentators dubbed the argument 'the Brezhnev doctrine'.*

47 Pravda
THE BREZHNEV DOCTRINE

In connection with the events in Czechoslovakia the question of the relationship and interconnection between the socialist countries' national interests and their internationalist obligations has assumed particular urgency and sharpness. The measures taken jointly by the Soviet Union and other socialist countries to defend the socialist gains of the Czechoslovak people are of enormous significance for strengthening the socialist commonwealth, which is the main achievement of the international working class.

At the same time it is impossible to ignore the allegations being heard in some places that the actions of the five socialist countries contradict the Marxist-Leninist principle of sovereignty and the right of nations to self-determination.

Such arguments are untenable primarily because they are

based on an abstract, non-class approach to the question of sovereignty and the right of nations to self-determination.

There is no doubt that the peoples of the socialist countries and the Communist parties have and must have freedom to determine their country's path of development. However any decision of theirs must damage neither socialism in their own country nor the fundamental interests of the other socialist countries nor the worldwide workers' movement, which is waging a struggle for socialism. This means that every communist party is responsible not only to its own people but also to all the socialist countries and to the entire communist movement. Whoever forgets this in placing sole emphasis on the autonomy and independence of communist parties lapses into one-sidedness, shirking his internationalist obligations.

The Marxist dialectic opposes one-sidedness; it requires that every phenomenon be examined in terms of both its specific nature and its overall connection with other phenomena and processes. Just as, in V.I. Lenin's words, someone living in a society cannot be free of that society, so a socialist state that is in a system of other states constituting a socialist commonwealth cannot be free of the common interests of that commonwealth ...

Each communist party is free in applying the principles of Marxism-Leninism and socialism in its own country, but it cannot deviate from these principles (if, of course, it remains a communist party). In concrete terms this means primarily that every communist party cannot fail to take into account in its activities such a decisive fact of our time as the struggle between the two antithetical social systems—capitalism and socialism. This struggle is an objective fact that does not depend on the will of people and is conditioned by the division of the world into two antithetical social systems ...

It should be stressed that even if a socialist country seeks to take an 'extra-block' position, it in fact retains its national independence thanks precisely to the power of the socialist commonwealth—and primarily to its chief force, the Soviet Union—and the might of its armed forces.

The weakening of any link in the world socialist system has a direct effect on all the socialist countries, which cannot be indifferent to this. Thus, the antisocialist forces in Czechoslovakia were in essence using talk about the right to self-determination to cover up demands for so-called neutrality and Czechoslovakia's withdrawal from the socialist commonwealth. But implementation of such 'self-determination' i.e. Czechoslovakia's separation from the socialist commonwealth, would run counter to Czechoslovakia's fundamental interests and would harm the other socialist countries. Such 'self-determination', as a result of which NATO troops might approach Soviet borders and the commonwealth of socialist countries would be dismembered, in fact infringes on the vital interests of these countries' peoples, and fundamentally contradicts the right of these peoples to socialist self-determination. The Soviet Union and other socialist states, in fulfilling their internationalist duty to the fraternal peoples of Czechoslovakia and defending their own socialist gains, had to act and did act in resolute opposition to the anti-socialist forces in Czechoslovakia . . .

SOURCE: 'Sovereignty and the International Obligations of Socialist Countries', by S. Kovalev in *Pravda* (26 September 1968); translated in *The Current Digest of the Soviet Press*, Vol XX, no 39 (16 October 1968). Translation Copyright 1973 by *The Current Digest of the Soviet Press*, published weekly at the Ohio State University by the American Association for the Advancement of Slavic Studies; reprinted by permission of the *Digest*

A few weeks later at the Polish Party Congress Leonid Brezhnev spelt out the idea in more pragmatic terms. He also elaborated on what he saw as capitalism's new emphasis on 'ideological subversion', a 'craftier tactic' of undermining socialism. This theme was to become a major preoccupation of Soviet and East European foreign policy in the next few years.

48 Leonid Brezhnev
ON 'SUBVERSION'

... The might of the socialist camp is now such that the imperialists fear a military rout in the event of a showdown with the main forces of socialism. Of course as long as imperialism exists, one cannot under any circumstances discount the danger of war with which imperialist policy is fraught. However, it is a fact that in the new conditions the imperialists more and more often resort to other, more crafty tactics. They seek weak links in the socialist front, follow a course of ideological subversion in the countries of socialism, endeavouring to influence the economic development of these countries, to try to sow discord, to drive wedges between them, to encourage and inflate nationalistic feelings and tendencies, and to seek to isolate one or another socialist state so as to seize them later by the throat one by one. In other words the imperialists try to wreck the stability of socialism precisely as a world system.

The experience of the socialist countries' struggle and development in these new conditions over recent years, including the activation not long ago of forces hostile to socialism in Czechoslovakia, brings home to Communists in the socialist countries with renewed force how important it is not to forget for a single moment certain vital time-tested truths.

If we do not want to slow down our progress on the road of socialist and communist construction, if we do not want to weaken our general positions in the struggle against imperialism, it is essential for us always and everywhere, in deciding any questions of our internal and external policy to preserve inviolate our loyalty to the principles of Marxism-Leninism, to display a clear-cut class and party approach to all social phenomena, and to give imperialism a resolute rebuff on the ideological front, making no concessions whatever to bourgeois ideology ...

The socialist countries stand for the strict respect of the sovereignty of all countries. We are strongly opposed to interference in the affairs of any states, and to the violation of their sovereignty . . . The Communist party of the Soviet Union has always been in favour of every socialist country determining the concrete forms of its development along the road to socialism, taking into account the specific character of its national conditions. But we know, comrades, that there are also general laws of socialist construction, deviations from which could lead to deviations from socialism as such. And when internal and external forces hostile to socialism try to turn the development of any socialist country backwards to a capitalist restoration, when a threat arises to the cause of socialism in that country, a threat to the security of the socialist community as a whole, that is no longer an issue only for the people of that country in question but a general issue which is the concern of all the socialist countries.

Obviously, such an action as military aid to a fraternal country in warding off a menace to the socialist system is an extraordinary, enforced measure that can be evoked only by direct actions on the part of the enemies of socialism within a country and outside it, actions which create a threat to the common interests of the socialist camp . . .

SOURCE: Leonid Brezhnev's speech at the Fifth Congress of the Polish United Workers' Party, Warsaw (12 November 1968), reprinted in *Following Lenin's Course: speeches and articles by L. I. Brezhnev* (Progress Publishers, Moscow 1972)

The invasion of Czechoslovakia caused a storm of outcry in the West, and even some repercussions in the Soviet Union. Like the Hungarian uprising in 1956, it coincided with a moment of crisis in the Western world, in this case the height of the protest movement against American policy in South Vietnam. It is impossible to say what weight the Soviet leadership placed on this in their calculations about the West's likely reaction. At all events, Western Governments did very little. Although President Johnson and his Secretary of State, Dean Rusk, expressed the ritual shock, their own policies in Vietnam gave them scant authority to condemn the invasion of Czechoslovakia. Within a few weeks their shock evaporated and President Johnson was trying to arrange a farewell summit meeting in Moscow before bowing out of the presidency in January 1969.

In the long run the way Western Communist parties reacted to the invasion was more important. The two largest parties, the French and the Italian, promptly condemned it, as did most of the smaller ones. The event cut one of the last remaining strings binding the Western parties to the Soviet Union.

In the Soviet Union the invasion evoked a number of protests, although it was only a minority that reacted. The silent majority was either uninterested and apathetic or else accepted that their Government was right. But within the small but growing movement of active dissidents the invasion of Czechoslovakia triggered off a new militancy.

With the slow awakening of Soviet Jewish interest in Israel, sparked off by the Six-Day War in 1967, a further strain of protest appeared. Over the next few years more and more Soviet Jews pushed for permission to emigrate, and were increasingly successful.

By the end of the second decade after Stalin's death several currents had merged into what was legitimately described abroad as the civil rights movement in the USSR. There was the intellectuals' movement, symbolised by Alexander Solzhenitsyn. It had a sub-branch of concerned scientists, led by Academician Andrei Sakharov, who had helped to build the first Soviet H-bomb and who later founded a 'Human Rights Committee'. There was the nationalities issue, symbolised by the Crimean Tatars and reflected in spasmodic protests in the Baltic republics and the Ukraine. Finally there was the Jewish movement, which was primarily a struggle not so much to change the system as to escape from it.

Interestingly, however, in contrast to the rest of Eastern Europe there was little evidence in the USSR of any current of reform within the Communist party itself. Nor were there any 'New Left' activists, criticising the Soviet system from a Marxist standpoint, as in Czechoslovakia, Hungary, or Poland. This phenomenon indicated that the Soviet Union was still very different from the rest of the area, more rigid and politically less changed.

On 30 April 1968 an underground and anonymous typesheet known as The Chronicle of Current Events *appeared in Moscow. It was a clandestine newsletter of the protest movement. For twenty-seven issues, at roughly two-monthly intervals, it continued to come out. Like other 'samizdat' documents, it was typed out in duplicate and passed from hand to hand until the secret police succeeded in suppressing it. The last issue was dated 15 October 1972. The third issue came out 10 days after the invasion of Czechoslovakia.*

49 The Chronicle of Current Events
SOVIET PROTEST

On 21 August 1968 the forces of five member countries of the Warsaw Pact carried out a treacherous and unprovoked attack on Czechoslovakia. The aggressive actions of the USSR and her allies met with a sharp rebuff from world public opinion. This issue of the *Chronicle* will deal with the events in our country which in one way or another are connected with the question of Czechoslovakia.

The facts show clearly that even in conditions which practic- ally preclude the possibility of resistance, the struggle for the realisation in practice of the principles of humanism and justice has not ceased . . . On 29 July a letter was handed in (by Grigorenko and Yakhimovich) to the Czechoslovak embassy, signed by five Soviet communists. It approved the new course of the Czechoslovak Communist party and condemned Soviet pressure on Czechoslovakia.

On 30 July Valery Pavlinchuk died. A young physicist from Obninsk, one of the most active and public-spirited people and communists in the city, a talented scientist and teacher, he was expelled from the party and dismissed from his work for circulating samizdat. Shortly before his death he sent an open letter to Alexander Dubcek, in which he directly expressed his solidarity with the new political course in Czechoslovakia, seeing it as an example of real socialist construction, free from dogmatism and excessive police control.

Even before the invasion, Czech newspapers had disappeared from the bookstalls, and with the invasion *L'Humanite*, *L'Unita*, the *Morning Star*, *Borba*, *Rinascita* and other publications ceased to arrive. Regular jamming of broadcasts from foreign radio stations began. The press and the ether were monopolised by our own propaganda.

On 24 August, in Moscow's October Square a certain citizen shouted out a slogan against the invasion of Czechoslovakia and was roughly beaten up by some strangers in plain clothes. Two of them hustled him into a car and drove off; the third remained beside a second car. Indignant onlookers began to demand that the police should detain this participant in the assault. But the police only examined his papers.

Many incidents are known of non-attendance on principle at meetings held with the aim of achieving unanimous approval for the sending of troops into Czechoslovakia. There have also been cases where people have found the courage either to refrain from voting or to vote against giving such approval . . .

Pamphlets containing protests against the occupation of Czechoslovakia have come to circulate widely in Moscow. The text of one of these documents is printed below.

'Let us think for ourselves'

The central committee and the majority of members of the Communist Party of China, also of the Communist parties of Albania, Indonesia, North Korea and the so-called parallel Communist parties of Japan, India and Australia declare that 'bourgeois revisionism' and open counter-revolution are triumphant in the USSR, that the Communist party of the Soviet Union, having unmasked the cult of Stalin and his crimes and not having recognised the genius of Mao, 'has betrayed the ideals of proletarian dictatorship', that 'the Soviet press slanders China', and so on.

But suppose a few of our ardent successors of Stalin and Beria suddenly decided to call on our Chinese, Albanian and other brothers to come to their aid?

What if the tanks and parachutists of these brothers suddenly appeared during the night in the streets of our towns? And if their soldiers, in the name of rescuing and defending the ideals of communism—as they understand them—began to arrest the leaders of our party and state, to close the newspapers, shut down the radio stations, and shoot those who dared to resist?

Not only the overwhelming majority of Czech and Slovak communists, but also the Italian, French, English, Swedish and Norwegian communists, in short the huge majority of communists of the whole world—among them the leaders of the 78 (out of 90) parties which have so far supported the Soviet party in its quarrel with the Chinese party—are convinced that after January 1968 Czechoslovakia had for the first time really begun to implement the ideas of Marx, and that in all our writings about 'counter-revolutionary threats' and 'revisionist degeneration' in Czechoslovakia there was not a single word of truth.

What if these foreign communists—and with them the great many people who think like them in Hungary, Poland, the G.D.R. and Bulgaria—communists who are convinced that the Soviet party is committing serious political errors, that the consequences of the Stalin cult have not only not been eliminated in our country but have even been considerably strengthened, and that the unprovoked military invasion of a peaceful socialist country bears witness to just this: supposing they all decided to 'rescue' us, and to set up in our country the type of socialism that they considered correct, with the help of tanks, guns, and parachutists?

What if there were to appear on the streets of our towns tanks and propagandists with machine-guns from Yugoslavia, Rumania, Czechoslovakia, and the G.D.R., and they were to begin to prove to us that this meant nothing but fraternal help and proletarian solidarity?

Let us think about this. Let us think whom all the events of August 21 have really helped, and whom they have harmed.

SOURCE: *Uncensored Russia*, the annotated text of the unofficial Moscow journal, *A Chronicle of Current Events*, Nos 1–11, edited and translated by Peter Reddaway (Jonathan Cape 1972)

PART FIVE

The Consumer
Revolution

One of the most significant features of the invasion of Czechoslovakia was the apathetic reaction in most of the rest of Eastern Europe. Apart from a handful of intellectuals in a few countries, almost no one protested. Most people shrugged their shoulders and asked 'What did the Czechs expect? Why didn't they learn from recent history?' In Poland and Hungary where 1956 was still remembered, this attitude was particularly strong.

One explanation is that in the period of almost 30 years of Eastern Europe's postwar history, people in the different countries have been kept politically apart. In spite of integration into Comecon and the Warsaw Pact, ordinary people have no real links with their neighbours. Only a relatively small proportion travels to other Eastern European countries. The languages are all different. The mass media give only scant coverage of neighbouring countries' affairs.

A second explanation is that the limits of political experimentation are now well known. Most people have learned to live with this as a fact of life. They have become interested in economic progress more than political change. By 1968 Hungary, in particular, was beginning to achieve a reasonable standard of living. Many Hungarians not only felt little sympathy with the Czechs but were even angry with them for 'rocking the boat' in a way which might have thrown everyone into the water.

The one place where the invasion of Czechoslovakia produced an intellectual outcry and reawakened a protest movement was the Soviet Union. It encouraged several dozen people—including writers, scientists, and performers—to launch a number of collective actions in opposition to official party policy. Andrei Sakharov, one of the builders of the Soviet hydrogen bomb, Mstislav Rostropovich, the world-famous cellist, and Alexander Solzhenitsyn were prominent in signing petitions which received publicity abroad. The underground publication, The Chronicle of Current Events, *set out to be a dossier on all the trials and other forms of harassment used by the authorities against the dissenters' movement.*

This movement grew in militancy after the Six-Day War in the Middle East, which revived the issue of Jewish emigration to Israel. Hundreds of Soviet Jews, though still only a small percentage of the 3 million Jews in the Soviet Union, took the risk of applying to leave the country. Their campaign merged partly with the rest of the intellectual opposition, and caused considerable embarrassment to the Soviet authorities. The KGB, the state security apparatus, became more active. Numerous people were sentenced to long terms in labour camps. Some leading dissenters were forcibly committed to mental hospitals. In 1973 in recognition of the importance of the issue, Yuri Andropov, the head of the KGB, was promoted to the Politburo. It was the first occasion since the time of Beria that the security police chief had a seat at the top.

This move towards repression was unique in Eastern Europe. Only in Czechoslovakia was there anything remotely resembling it. There, as a consequence of the invasion and particularly after Gustav Husak had replaced Alexander Dubcek as party leader in April 1969, a series of purges emptied the party of all its liberals. In the universities, the trade unions and the mass media thousands of people lost their jobs and found it impossible to get alternative work. But very few were imprisoned. In 1971 nineteen young Marxists were imprisoned, and in the summer of 1972 forty-six other socialists, including some prominent figures from 1968, were gaoled for trying to organise a protest campaign against the elections held the previous autumn. Elsewhere in Eastern Europe the intellectual climate, though still under central control, was considerably easier.

Two years after the invasion of Czechoslovakia there came a different upheaval, this time in Poland. It produced unambiguous benefits for

Eastern Europe. A fortnight before Christmas the Polish Government raised food prices by approximately 30 per cent. In the Baltic ports of Gdansk and Szczecin shipyard workers were already suspicious of a new wage system which was due to start in January and which many thought would effectively mean a cut in living standards. The food price increase was the last straw. They went on strike.

The Government over-reacted. Three days of demonstrations which threatened to spread all over Poland ended in the toppling of Mr Gomulka. The Soviet Union did nothing to save him. The events had an enormous impact all over Eastern Europe.

In the Soviet Union, Rumania, Bulgaria and East Germany governments adjusted the Five-year plans which were about to be settled for 1971–5. New investments were put into the production of consumer goods and into housing. The lowest paid workers received wage increases. Governments seemed to conclude that the best way to achieve a national consensus and win popular support was to convince people that extra work would bring immediate rewards. The old philosophy had tended to be that investment now would benefit the next generation rather than the present one. From 1970 onwards the time scale shifted. Consumers were promised a more rapid increase in their standard of living. The policy chimed in with the popular mood, which was for high mass consumption. Like other industrial societies, Eastern Europe's nations had passed through a generation of postwar reconstruction. They now wanted to enjoy the fruits of a stable, secure, and comfortable existence. The restrictions on intellectual freedom were accepted as an irksome burden, but in the light of material improvements in the standard of living most people found them tolerable.

Enormous changes have occurred in the social structure of every Eastern European nation. Agrarian countries have been industrialised. Rural populations have emigrated to the cities. There is universal education and admirable medical services. The political system is still highly centralised and authoritarian, but it is better able to acknowledge different interest groups than in Stalin's day.

The difference between top and bottom incomes is still comparatively narrow, at least outside the Soviet Union. The USSR's longer history has produced a more rigid social structure of a new type, with considerable regional differences of income still and a wider gap between top and bottom. In Eastern Europe, just as the political system is more relaxed, so is there less of a closed ruling elite.

What kind of societies are these? To many observers in the West the key factor is the political system. Its centralised, authoritarian nature distinguishes it from the one which prevails in Western Europe. To leftwing critics in the West and to some in Eastern Europe too (see Document 38) these are societies which claim to represent the working class and in which the working class has little power. The fact that workers are living better than ever before is less important than the emergence of a meritocracy which virtually monopolises political and economic power, even though access to it is open to the children of workers and peasants.

Both lines of argument tend to ignore the non-political aspects of Eastern European life. These societies can now be seen as a particular, centralised variant of the welfare state. Their Governments consider it their natural duty to use state control to provide adequate educational and welfare services. Although the practice of making political appointments survives in parts of the system, access to responsible positions depends mainly on education, and educational opportunities are not unfairly distributed. Eastern European societies show high upward mobility for the ambitious, the educated, and the hardworking. Most Europeans, in the West and in the East, accept this as the correct order of things. Politics are not a major day-to-day preoccupation. People live, as they do in most societies, for the simpler goals of security and comfort. In a way that was inconceivable 21 years ago when Stalin died, these goals can now be satisfied in Eastern Europe.

The Polish disturbances on the Baltic coast in December 1970 began as demonstrations and ended in riots and bloodshed. Shipyard workers marching through the streets singing the Internationale were confronted by militiamen and violence broke out. In 3 days of clashes scores of people died.

The scandal of this misguided and brutal reaction was enough to show the bankruptcy of Gomulka's leadership. He was replaced by Edward Gierek, who immediately promised the workers reforms although he refused to cancel the food price increases which had caused the original outcry.

A month later workers in Szczecin mounted a potentially far more threatening action against the new leadership. This time they stopped work but remained in the shipyards. They declared that they would not resume work until food prices came down again. Unlike his predecessor Gomulka, Gierek decided to take the steam out of the situation by risking a personal confrontation with the strikers. He went up to Szczecin and addressed the workers in the shipyards. The dialogue was effective and the strikers went back. But their meeting with Gierek showed the extent of their militancy and, at the same time, their willingness to put their trust in the party leadership again.

50 Polish Workers
CONFRONTATION WITH EDWARD GIEREK

Delegate of the NTP Department: Workers of the Shipyards! I speak in the name of NTP. First, I would like to say: Comrade Gierek, you talk of a change. Do you know what a change is? It's the fact that we are here. (Shouts, applause, ovations.) We who are workers, Communists, and for People's Poland. So, it's with us that you should hold discussions, instead of sending the militia after us as if we were bandits, instead of surrounding us with a cordon of troops and trying to starve us out by preventing food from reaching us during the strike . . .

Comrade Gierek, in the morning after this long night, we'll go back to work, but we want before that to have some honest and direct answers. We've been lied to too much. Not by you, perhaps, Comrade Gierek, but by the others . . . Well, now we want the central committee to commit itself and take a position on this affair. We want . . .

Gierek: That I cannot accept! It's an ultimatum . . . (Stirring and anger in the hall) after all, I'm not the central committee. I'm only the First Secretary. It's up to the committee to decide . . .

Delegate from the NTP: That's true. Comrade Gierek is

right; he cannot answer all by himself. Do you know what that
means? That means that the days of the cult of personality are
over, workers! Hurray for Comrade Gierek . . . (Applause and
laughter) But before I finish I want to say that we've waited
25 years for this historic moment. Now, today, in the presence
of the Government and of the Comrade First Secretary we
want everything—yes, everything that has been said here—to
be put in black and white. No traps! Thank you.

Delegate from SGW: I'm from SGW. I've got a question for
the central committee: do we punish criminals in our country,
or do we pay them? Someone answer me. We Poles punished
the Germans for their crimes . . . for shooting at us. Let the
First Secretary of the central committee give me the answer: are
crimes punished or rewarded?

Gierek: Don't force me to answer like that, or I won't answer
you.

Delegate from SGW: Now, second point. Retirement. The
retirement age ought to be 60 and not 65. We should also
revise the work categories and modify the shipyard worksheets
. . . As for the demands, I'll say we've discussed them with the
workers. They agree to suspend the strike and go back to work
on Monday. Thanks . . . and I greet the new central committee
and the Government. In the name of the workers! (Applause).

Delegate from DZ: Esteemed citizens! I am non-party, and
this is the seventeenth year that I have worked in the yards.
It so happens that I am on the strike committee. I listened to
comrade Gierek's speech and, believe me, it brought tears to
my eyes. Comrade Gierek particularly emphasised our country's
difficult economic situation. My section and I support him, and
we will end the strike. But we say urgently to the Comrade
Secretary and our new Government: we're at the end of our
strength! Because, frankly, we earn very little, and we hope
the Government is going to do all it can to ensure that, within
the next few months, the working class will be able to raise its
standard of living. We are good workers, but if we see that
something of this sort is being done, then we'll work even harder.

We genuinely want unity between us. Thank you (Applause).

A Delegate: I still have to give the final answer of the workers in my department on ending the strike. Comrade Gierek! I'm an old party member. I only want to tell the truth. I don't want to disguise the situation nor do I want to blacken my department. I don't want to be misunderstood. When I arrived, the situation in the department was as follows: a unanimous reply of 'We want to go on with the strike!' That was the decision. After a long and stormy discussion we reached a conclusion: we can't carry on alone as a department. I don't want to urge the shipyards to continue with the strike, that's not my aim. But I would like to draw attention to the fact that the workers in our department are critical of all those who spoke before me, who they understood to have given way too easily on the question of cancelling the increase in food prices . . . and this despite the fact that throughout the strike, not one dignitary showed up to intervene and try to convince us of the justice of this measure. Moreover, our department believes that in coming out on strike we, the naval shipyard workers, caused other enterprises to come out. Now this demand is not being met, and we're not living up to the trust they place in us. Comrade Gierek, I'm speaking the truth. The workers in our department have not been convinced by your remarks . . . and I'd like to say this: we'll stop the strike, not through conviction, but because the others are stopping. That's all.

President of the Strike Committee: We demand full, correct information on the political and economic situation in the shipyards and in the country . . . Gentlemen, colleagues, and comrades, it's quite obvious: the Government will never be either popular or democratic as long as . . . the Government is aware, I believe, that information is an element, an area, of the greatest importance! Remember the German hangman, Goebbels. Do you remember that he was the pillar of Hitlerism? What about us? But we have a people's state; this strength is among us! This press, this fine radio station built with our own hands, the microphone in front of me, the television, the

N

newspapers, the very paper they're printed on—none of this should be directed against us. Against our interests. On the contrary they ought to make our life pleasanter. They should inform! Bring together! Unite! Well, they don't because until now these things have to a large extent been thrown into the dustbin. They were simply wasted—not used.

We demand that our claims be published in the local mass media before 25 January 1971. Comrades, citizens, colleagues: this business must be reported. We are not insubstantial, we exist, and we're not going to give way on this point.

We demand that the security services immediately stop harassing, threatening and arresting workers taking part in the strike. The strike is not an offence, for nothing in our laws forbids it. I'd like to underline one thing here. We have repeatedly demanded: the law must be respected. That's why I'm not going to enlarge on it now.

I believe—I demand in the name of the workers—that in the end Comrade Gierek, or someone in the Government will have to answer us; and that in the end they will give us a few words more of hope and reassurance. For that is the only way that everyone can be entirely satisfied with what has been accomplished. Thank you . . .

SOURCE: 'Polish Workers and Party Leaders: a Confrontation', the transcript of a meeting held in the Adolf Warski shipyard in Szczecin in January 1971. Full text published by SELIO 87, rue du Faubourg St Denis, Paris; in English in *New Left Review*, no 72 (March/April 1972), reprinted by permission of *New Left Review*

The Soviet Union held its Twenty-fourth Party Congress 3 months after the Polish strikes and riots. Obviously their impact on the rest of Eastern Europe was not officially acknowledged. A trend towards improving the supply and quality of consumer goods was already visible for some time before riots, but it is indisputable that the events in Poland accelerated it. In his report to the Soviet Congress Leonid Brezhnev stressed the shift towards consumer goods production. He argued the case both for its own sake and as a way of improving the productivity of Soviet workers and of the economy as a whole.

51 Leonid Brezhnev
THE SWITCH TO CONSUMER GOODS

The central committee proposes that the main task in the ninth Five-Year Plan should be a substantial rise in the prosperity of working people. It intends this policy to define not only our activity in the next five years but also the general orientation of the country's longterm economic development. The party assumes firstly that the highest aim of social production under socialism is fully to satisfy people's material and cultural needs. From the first days of Soviet rule our party and state has done everything they could in that direction. However, for a long period our possibilities, for well-known historical reasons, were restricted. Now they have been substantially extended. And this gives the party grounds for raising the issue of aiming economic construction even more towards improving people's standard of living.

The party also proceeds on the assumption that greater prosperity for working people will continue to become an urgent requirement of our economic development, in fact one of the vital economic prerequisites for rapid growth . . . This approach not only follows from our aim of developing the role of material and moral incentives to work. It is part of a much broader context: the creation of favourable conditions for developing the capabilities and constructive activity of all working people who are society's main productive force. Modern production imposes rapidly growing demands, not so much on machines as on workers themselves and those who design the machines and control the equipment.

Specialist knowledge, a high degree of professional training, and a man's general cultural level are becoming essential to successful work by increasingly broad sections of the country's workers. But it depends very much on their standard of living and on how fully their material and spiritual needs can be satisfied. Thus our aims, that is the increase of our economic potential as well as the fulfilment of the requirements of a developing economy, make it possible and essential to achieve a more profound switch towards raising living standards. . . .

Comrades, during the last five years the production and sale of industrial consumer goods has grown substantially. Nevertheless even today the production of many articles lags behind demand. The increase we propose in workers' cash incomes will raise demand further and pose the problem of quality more sharply. Is our industry ready to meet the requirements of party policy in raising living standards? In terms of the objective possibilities it is undoubtedly ready. The country's industrial potential is enough to ensure a considerable growth in output and an improvement in the quality of consumer goods.

Our greater possibilities allow us to invest more capital in this direction—and this is what we are doing. But success is not only determined by the objective conditions. Subjective factors also matter enormously. The central committee believes it is important to remind the planning organs, and the party, administrative, and trade union organisations of the need to change the approach towards producing consumer goods.

Behind us, comrades, are long years of heroic history when millions of Communists and nonparty citizens conscientiously accepted considerable deprivations, were ready to make do with bare necessities, and did not consider it their right to demand special comforts. This was bound to affect the output, quality, and range of consumer goods. But what was explicable and natural in the past when other tasks had the main priority, is not acceptable now.

We still have workers, not only locally but at the centre too, who manage to live happily with shortcomings and who have somehow got used to low quality in a number of consumer goods. Their output develops intolerably slowly. Other workers stop producing essential items altogether under the pretext of replacing obsolete products with new ones; they take cheap items out of production even though they are essential for the population. That is how shortages of supposedly less important goods occur. But they certainly cannot be less important when they are in daily demand.

In the next five-year period we can substantially improve the supply of consumer goods. The output of fabrics, clothing, footwear and knitwear is planned to rise considerably. As for durables such as television sets, refrigerators, radios, and washing machines, we can really get near the target of fully satisfying the population's needs. There will be a large increase in car sales; in 1975 they will be three times as high as in 1970. The solution of such tasks is now fully within our capacity; we only have to use our potential and our reserves as fully as possible . . .

Source: The BBC Monitoring Service's Summary of World Broadcasts, SU/3649/C/1, reprinted by permission of the BBC

The ruler who best exemplifies a realistic and modern attitude in Eastern Europe is Janos Kadar, the Hungarian party leader. He was installed in power in 1956 when the Russian tanks crushed the uprising. But from this inauspicious beginning and with the original reputation of a traitor, Kadar has worked his way to a position now of considerable respect among his countrymen.

He has done it mainly by his self-effacing style of leadership and his early recognition that economic progress is the country's chief priority. On his sixtieth birthday Kadar made an impromptu speech at a luncheon given in his honour. It provided an unusually revealing glimpse of his philosophy of life.

52 Janos Kadar
LIFE IS A COMPROMISE

What is the course of a person's life like? I believe if one has in mind here not merely a vegetable life, but human life in the noblest sense of the word, then the first point is that one should understand you must succeed and struggle in life for your place in the sun, not as an individual, but by recognising that in human terms you cannot find happiness by yourself but only together with others . . .

I consider myself lucky that I came across socialism and the Marxist-Leninist ideology. I became acquainted with this ideology and it took hold of me. And—maybe you will not misunderstand me when I say without boasting—that in a critical period of my life I reached the point, though not without assistance, where I understood that if I wanted to be a happy and free human being, free in person and free in spirit, I could not do this on my own, but only in company with the working class and my comrades in this class, only if I strove for an even better understanding of this socialist ideology and range of ideals, and all the more so if I lived according to it. And this is the true merit of an individual. Everything else, I should like to stress, depends on other factors and not on the determination of the individual.

Without any ideology or ideals, a person cannot live a human life as an individual and a social being . . . I know other countries which are richer, in the material sense, than we are and yet their social system has no future, because they have no ideology which leads them forward. Therefore I believe it is fortunate for a person to have an ideology for which he can work . . .

As a small child I lived in the country. Later, I came to the city and became an industrial worker, and a Communist. There is a piece of wisdom which one hears from older people as early as the age of five; older people tell children that reason and common sense are extremely important. I believe that this is true. As I have said before, an ideology and an ideal which can guide a person are essential. Otherwise you cannot progress in a direction useful for society.

Some people profess Christianity or some other ideology as their ideal. I am partial. I believe that Marxism-Leninism is the best ideological system. But in any case, an ideology is essential; common human awareness and a sense of reality . . .

I might divulge here, as there are some older people amongst us, that life is in many ways a compromise. Nothing ever comes about in the way one believes it will at the beginning. Back in the olden days, I was already dreaming about liberation, socialism, and communism, and although there was no certainty then that I would ever live to see the day of liberation, it was clear to me even then that when that day arrived, a few government regulations would be issued and socialism would materialise. This was a quarter of a century ago, and as it turns out things did not happen in quite that way. Life therefore forced us in a certain sense to compromise, but in the good sense of the word. What we need is not retrogressive compromise but decisions which take into consideration the real situation and which help us to go forward toward our ideals and goals.

Our Marxist-Leninist Weltanschauung is a scientific ideological system which guides our social life. But it cannot be contrary to the rational human mind. Our theory has to be more than the rational human mind but it cannot come into conflict with it because if it does then it is no longer Marxism-Leninism or a communist doctrine, and something is wrong. We have therefore a system of thinking which we call dialectical materialism according to which social life and nature too have their dialectics. Everyone knows that dialectics are more than logic. But one of my practical philosophies—if I may use the term—is that I have discovered that dialectics cannot conflict with logic: therefore it has to be logical too because if it is not, it cannot be dialectical either.

I could enumerate a few other such lessons I have learnt. My deep conviction is that the humanism of our age consists of Marxism-Leninism as a science, and of communism as an ideology. This means decency, integrity, and humaneness, and its objective is the improvement of human life. At times I say that the relationship between Marxism-Leninism, socialism, and communism on the one hand and the Hungarian working class and the Hungarian people on the other, does not consist of the fact that we possess an excellent theory which we are trying out on ten million guinea pigs. I believe it is the other way round; Marxism-Leninism and the entire communist ideological system exist for the purpose of giving these ten million Hungarians a better life. For if it were not there for this purpose, and something were wrong in this respect, we would not be doing a good job. I am very glad that recognition of this is increasingly gaining ground in our country and people representing Marxism-Leninism are becoming ever more infused by a sense of reality and humaneness, by a regard for and an appreciation of non-communists, and the resulting awareness that we can only progress together . . .

SOURCE: Janos Kadar's birthday speech (25 May 1972), published in *Tarsadalmi Szemle* (June 1972)

Life has changed immeasurably in the rural areas of Eastern Europe since the war. In every country except Poland and Yugoslavia the dominant form of agriculture is the cooperative farm. The two commonest prewar patterns of landholding, the large private estate and the small private farm, have disappeared.

And yet the nature of ownership is less important than the other changes. Even Poland and Yugoslavia, which have continued with private peasant farming, are part of the mainstream in most respects. Agriculture is more mechanised than ever. Welfare services have been extended to the villages. The cities are attracting more and more young people off the land. The quiet of the countryside is broken by the chugging sound of mopeds and motorcycles. Many young countrypeople combine life in the village with work in the town. They are 'worker-peasants', travelling daily to nearby factories or building sites while living on farms and helping out on occasional evenings or during harvest time. These trends towards modernisation and urbanisation have been going on, almost regardless of the political set-up at the top. They form part of the basic landscape of Eastern Europe.

One of the best accounts of the process was written by two Hungarian ethnographers working on a joint Hungarian and American academic project. They examined the changes over a period of years in a small village in Eastern Hungary called Atany. Their findings formed part of the publications of a research series edited at the University of Chicago.

53 Edit Fel and Tamas Hofer
THE CHANGE IN PEASANT LIFE

Our field work was begun at a relatively fortunate time. By February, 1951, the damages from World War II were more or less repaired and the peasant farms were profitable. Both the exteriors and the interiors of the snow-covered rural houses followed 'the Atany custom,' as did the attire of the men and women. Women and girls were spinning and weaving in the houses. The males gathered in the stables to talk. At sunset one could observe the men returning to their homes from the distant fields, carrying bundles of straw for fuel on their backs. On Sundays the church was crowded, and the villages sang the psalms with visible satisfaction. National leadership was in the hands of the Hungarian Workers' Party, a Communist government which aimed to reorganize the country according to socialist principles. However, at the level of the local villages, the measures had not affected the majority of the populace. Only a few rich farmers and the church had to hand over their land to the state. The school had been nationalized and the system of village administration had been altered.

In several regions of Europe the rural way of life is but a damaged and diluted vestige of former times; in other regions the peasants themselves feel that it is a burden which has been forced on them and almost suffocates them. Unlike these groups, our Atany informants professed themselves peasants with pleasure and pride. This is the portrait of a Hungarian village during the moments preceding fundamental change, when the institutions were still living and working, but when they were no longer taken for granted as in former times. It was a time when the people were especially conscious of their traditional

o

way of life and sometimes saw it in the rose-coloured light of
their attachment.

Today this portrait is no longer typical of Atany. It has
become a historical document. Events followed each other
rapidly. With the compulsory delivery of agricultural products
to the state, which was increased from year to year, all peasant
economies have in effect been subjected to a strict state supervision. The Government's programme to annihilate the social
stratum of well-to-do farmers as such has also been realised at
Atany. Their houses were confiscated, and several were imprisoned. In 1952-53 the situation was made worse by an
especially poor harvest, so that even the basic subsistence of
men and animals became irregular.

In the autumn of 1951 the first co-operative farms were
founded; at that time they were primarily associations for the
common execution of certain specified tasks. The membership
of the co-operative farms varied widely during the following
years, owing to changes in the policy of the government and
alterations of the burdens weighing on 'private' farms, but it
never included more than a small fraction of the population.
The general collectivization of the Hungarian peasantry was
begun in 1958; Atany's turn came in February, 1959. All the
fields were put under the management of the co-operative
farms, except for 160 acres which remained private property.

The co-operative farms practice a mixed agriculture similar
to that of the peasants; they still raise grain and breed animals.
However, ploughing is done with tractors, as is much of the
harvest in dry years, when combines are able to work in the
fields. There are hardly any horses in the village now. The
co-operatives pay some rent to the old owners in proportion to
their former acreage, but the main income of the members is
the share which they receive on the basis of the work they
actually perform, calculated in workday units and paid in kind
and in cash. The co-operative reallots about one and a third
acres of land to each member family. The income derived from
intensive cultivation of this plot and from livestock raising in

private stables nearly equals the income received directly from the co-operative.

Since the beginning of the 1950s the extended families have dissolved rapidly, owing to the burden of progressive taxation and compulsory delivery of agricultural products to the state. Most of these 'dissolutions' were purely formal, a smaller number were actual. The traditional organization of labour by families has become extinct in the co-operatives; the members of a family are assigned to different brigades and tasks, according to their age and sex. More and more of the young people turn to industry for employment and move to the towns permanently. The average age of the co-operative membership is 57 years.

The weight of recent events has produced rapid modernization and urbanization of the Atany peasantry. Young persons from the village are now able to adjust easily to an urban environment. Modernization and urbanization have produced many notable benefits for the villagers in the form of better health standards, schooling, ease of communication, and manufactured goods. However, the transition has been possible only at the expense of the traditional way of life.

The goals which motivated the efforts of the Atany people in the old days—the acquisition of land and fine animals and the finding of a self-sufficient farm for one's successors—have lost their meaning. Not only in the material sphere, but also in other respects, the old homogeneous order has disappeared. New houses are built, no longer in the 'Atany way', but following allegedly urban models, and often replacing old buildings in good condition and suitable for living in. Mass-produced furniture, radios, and sometimes television sets are seen in the living rooms. In 1958 a cultural centre and a new school building were constructed, and eight years of schooling are now obligatory. The members of the co-operative farms are entitled to medical treatment at reduced rates, and many of them take advantage of it. Babies are born at the maternity centre at Heves, but the birth rate is extremely low. The old restrictions on marriage and the choice of spouse are gone; young men who work in the towns often do not look for a Calvinist wife, and the young woman is no longer placed under the guidance of her mother-in-law in order to learn the Atany customs. The increased demands on people's time and the altered daily schedule leave hardly any chance to cultivate good relations with kinsmen or members of one's age group. The kin group assembles only for the large family ceremonies, the weddings and funerals. Church life is likewise restricted to special holidays; on these days the church is full, but hardly anyone attends the Sunday services.

The young people of Atany dream of learning a craft, of becoming industrial workers, or even 'educated people' so as to receive weekly or monthly wages and retirement pay in their old age. The older people try to find a place in the changing Atany world; they have become uncertain, lacking the support of the traditional order. They get their wheat allowance from the co-operative farm, and most of them bake their bread at home, but this wheat is not the same as the wheat they used to grow themselves in the old days. As a former rich farmer put it, 'We don't know when it was sown, or the time when it was reaped; the wheat is just brought. One feels there is no summer anymore. In the old days we saw that people were harvesting, meals were being carried out to the fields for the reapers, the crop was gathered in, carts went and returned, stacks were piled in every yard. Now everything is all alike. It seems as if we were not in the same world where we used to live'.

SOURCE: 'Proper Peasants: Traditional Life in a Hungarian Village', by Edit Fel and Tamas Hofer, Viking Fund Publications in *Anthropology*, no 46, distributed through the Wenner-Gren Foundation for Anthropological Research, Inc; part of a series edited by Professor Sol Tax, Chicago University, published by the Aldine Publishing Company, Chicago, Illinois

More than half the population of Eastern Europe is too young to have any memories of life during or before the war. Their whole experience has been of centralised socialism. Their attitudes and aspirations, however, seem broadly similar to those of their counterparts in the West.

After two decades of cold war propaganda on both sides of the mythical Iron Curtain, the outlook of the new generation in Eastern Europe is easily comprehensible to its Western contemporaries. The rival clichés may characterise Eastern Europe as a collectivised hell and Western Europe as a jungle inhabited by competing individuals. But the facts show that a real dialogue between the two halves of Europe would present no difficulty.

A Polish study published in the winter of 1972 gave an illuminating picture of young Poles' hopes and ambitions. It could equally well have applied to young Hungarians, Rumanians, or Czechs—or for that matter to Frenchmen, Swedes, or the English.

54 W. Adamski
YOUNG PEOPLE—1971

The Institute of Youth Studies in the Higher School of the Social Sciences has completed work on a poll entitled 'Young People—1971'. This sociological study has found a rare response among the younger generation. The institute collected 12,000 completed questionnaires and about 2,000 extensive answers . . .

What are the special characteristics of young people in the early 1970's? What are their ambitions in life and their social aspirations? A comparison between the results of the poll and earlier findings is only partly possible and not merely because of the scattered and interrupted nature of the studies involved, which has been so characteristic of this country. A source of frequently insurmountable difficulties encountered by anyone who wished to reconstruct a comprehensive intellectual profile of youth in the past few decades lies above all in the one-sided interest of researchers in the past . . . Little attention was paid to the value of youth's possible or actual contributions to social development.

The year 1971 is an unusual one in the postwar history of our country. And the young people whose portrait is presented here are also unusual. As in the economy or social life, they display—along with similarities and continuity—symptoms which must have been maturing in secret for some time, but which have now emerged with exceptional force.

The generally expressed ambition of young people in 1971 is to found a family, as a haven of love and of the harmonious joint life of a married couple, and as a source of joy from their children. The largest group among the young people in the study would like to direct its long-range efforts to this goal. On the average one out of every four respondents selected this 'family-oriented' goal as superior to the others available.

Others selected in statistical order the following social values as their main goal and inspiration:

1. The desire to obtain a college degree, coinciding partly with the need for a constant improvement in knowledge;

2. Response to various aspects of social prestige, mainly apparent in social or political activity; among those who professed this aim, we find both individuals who find satisfaction in influencing other people and the course of social events, and those who act mainly out of an internal need to be 'socially useful';

3. A desire to become highly qualified and to obtain an outstanding position in one's profession or trade;

4. Fascination with material wealth, combined with a strong desire for security, guaranteed by a well-furnished house and an 'easy life'. Each of the above groups includes 'family happiness' as an accompanying value . . .

Can the aspirations and desires of young people come true? When asked: 'Do you believe that you will be able to achieve your goals?' two-thirds of the respondents answered strongly in the affirmative, and only one per cent answered in the negative. . . .

SOURCE: 'Young People—1971', by W. Adamski, in the Warsaw daily paper *Życie Warszawy* (22–3 October 1972)

Epilogue

On 5 March 1973, the twentieth anniversary of Stalin's death, there was not a single mention of the event in *Pravda* or any other newspaper in Eastern Europe—except one. For an area which religiously commemorates all kinds of anniversaries the silence was remarkable.

The one exception was Albania where on its front page the party daily *Zeri i Populit* claimed in an editorial that 'all revolutionaries and freedom-loving peoples remember J. V. Stalin as a great revolutionary and as an outstanding Marxist-Leninist'. 'By now', the article went on, 'the leaders of the Soviet Union and the other revisionists in some former socialist countries have cut all the threads binding them to Marxism-Leninism . . . and have restored capitalism.'

Pravda's front page on that day was a revealing contrast. The editorial was headed 'The Technical Creativity of Millions' and praised the Soviet Union's scientific progress. There were two pictures: one was of Angarsk, a new town built alongside a giant petro-chemical complex, and the other of tea-pickers in Georgia. The main news story was about the spring sowing. It was a routine and humdrum day.

Two months later a Politburo meeting ratified the most important switch in Soviet foreign policy for 20 years and the final burial of the cold-war strategy of all-out East-West confrontation, symbolised on the Soviet side by Stalin's ruthless posture.

The Politburo endorsed Mr Brezhnev's forthcoming visits to West Germany and the United States, and the policy of close cooperation with the West. The whole picture of global power has changed. President Nixon's visit to Peking in February 1972 confirmed the fact that China is now a decisive factor in international politics. His summit meeting in Moscow and the establishment of regular top-level US-Soviet consultations put the two countries' relations on a new and different level.

Washington recognised Moscow's right to 'parity' in nuclear weapons. In June 1973 the two powers agreed to consult each other urgently whenever a threat to peace arose anywhere in the world, a move which came near to setting up a US-Soviet condominium to police the planet. Washington and Moscow have decided that peace can best be guaranteed if they lock themselves into a system of long-term relationships which either side will find it too costly to destroy.

The political bargain is being given flesh by massive economic deals. In return for access to Western advanced technology and, where necessary, to food supplies, the Soviet Union is opening up its deposits of oil, natural gas, and copper to Western capital.

The USSR's split with China has clearly helped to change Moscow's policy. By playing the China card, President Nixon encouraged the Soviet Union to seek out a new relationship with the USA. Partly in order to upstage Peking, and partly to ensure that the US-China link did not disrupt the USSR's own relations with Washington, the Soviet leaders felt compelled to enter into the long-term bargain with the United States. International relations are infinitely more complex now. Alongside the new arch of US-Soviet relations there are now three other centres of power, China, Japan, and Western Europe. The brutal simplicity of Stalin's world is dead and buried.

Suggestions for Further Reading

The best general introduction to the period since Stalin's death is François Fejtö's *A History of the People's Democracies: Eastern Europe since Stalin* (1971). It deals with the period in two halves, first chronologically and then in terms of issues. Other useful books on the 'people's democracies' are J. F. Brown's *The New Eastern Europe: the Khruschev Era and After* (1966) and *Eastern Europe in the Sixties* (1963), edited by S. Fischer-Galati. George Schöpflin's edited handbook *The Soviet Union and Eastern Europe* (1970) is a valuable collection of essays which lays special stress on the institutional framework and describes how trade unions, the educational system, the law, etc, function.

Two books which discuss the social stratification of Eastern European societies in some depth are David Lane's *The End of Inequality?* (1971) and Frank Parkin's *Class, Inequality, and Social Order* (1972). This is still a rather neglected field, but David Lane in *Politics and Society in the USSR* (1970) has attempted to do the same kind of analysis for the Soviet Union. For a more polemical analysis of Soviet and Eastern European political and social systems Milovan Djilas' *The New Class* (1966), Kuron & Modzelewski's *Open Letter to the Party* (1968), and Andrei Amalrik's *Will the Soviet Union Survive until 1984?* (1969) are useful.

Leonard Shapiro's *The Government and Politics of the Soviet Union* (second edition, 1967) is a clear and incisive introduction to the Soviet system. Another book which ought not to be overlooked is Michel Tatu's *Power in the Kremlin: from Khruschev's decline to collective leadership* (1969). This is one of the best pieces of 'Kremlinology' ever written, an attempt at reconstructing the way groups and cliques within the Politburo and central committee formed and re-formed during the 1960s.

On the Soviet economy three important books are Abram Bergson's *The Economics of Soviet Planning* (1964), Alec Nove's *The Soviet Economy* (revised edition, 1968) and Philip Hanson's *The Consumer in the Soviet Economy* (1968).

Numerous books deal with Soviet foreign policy, and any specific listing must be highly selective. For a straightforward journalistic account the best place to go is to André Fontaine's *History of the Cold War*, vol II (1970), which covers the period from 1953 to 1963. D. F. Fleming's *The Cold War and its Origins* (1961) is important. For two diametrically opposed versions of a still very controversial period there are D. J. Dallin's *Soviet Foreign Policy after Stalin* (1962), which takes the line that Soviet policy was aggressive and expansionist; and David Horowitz's *From Yalta to Vietnam* (1965), which puts the main onus for the cold war on the United States. Isaac Deutscher's *The Great Contest: Russia and the West* (1960) is illuminating, and the same author's *Russia, China, and the West* (1970) is the best account of the growing split between China and the Soviet Union. Although it is a collection of articles and commentaries written as the events unfolded, it loses nothing by hindsight. Deutscher had an unusual perception of the long-term trends behind the manoeuvrings between Moscow and Peking.

The various crises in the course of de-Stalinisation have been extensively treated. For Hungary, 1956, Tibor Meray's *Thirteen Days that Shook the Kremlin* (1959) and François Fejtö's *Behind the Rape of Hungary* (1957) give full accounts. Konrad Syrop's *Spring in October* (1957) deals with Poland, 1956. The Prague spring of 1968 has, by now, an enormous literature.

The most readable and best informed analysis is probably Pavel Tigrid's *Why Dubcek Fell* (1971).

Undoubtedly the best introduction to the Balkan states of Eastern Europe is Paul Lendvai's *Eagles in Cobwebs: Nationalism and Communism in the Balkans* (1969), which covers Albania, Bulgaria, Rumania and Yugoslavia. Lendvai has also written a useful study in *Anti-semitism in Eastern Europe* (1972), which is the best piece of work on this subject, even though its title is a little ambitious. The book mainly deals with anti-semitism within the Communist parties rather than in the societies at large. Finally, on a general topic, Paul Neuburg's *The Hero's Children* gives a convincing description of the attitudes of the young generations in Eastern Europe.

Acknowledgements

My thanks are due to all those who allowed me to reprint
material for which they own the copyright. In particular they
include the American Association for the Advancement of
Slavic Studies, who publish *The Current Digest of the Soviet Press*,
the British Broadcasting Corporation, the Columbia University
Press, Victor Gollancz Ltd, Granada Publishing Ltd, the
Harvill Press Ltd, the Institute of Jewish Affairs, *International
Socialism*, Leszek Kolakowski, Macdonald & Company Ltd,
New Left Review, Praeger Publishers Inc, and Peter Reddaway.
I should also like to thank my wife, Ruth, for enduring
tedious evenings while I sat at a typewriter and for helping
out during my absences in Eastern Europe.

Index

Abakumov, V. S., 44
Adamski, W., 205ff
Agriculture, 15, 129
  in Czechoslovakia, 15–16
  in Hungary, 15–16, 35ff, 57, 62, 200
  in Poland, 10, 15 16, 78, 81
Albania
  break with Moscow, 87, 99ff, 120, 185
  economic growth, 129
  relations with Yugoslavia, 28ff
  respect for Stalin, 207
Andropov, Y., 188
Apro, A., 58ff

Bacilek, K., 158
Bem, J., 65
Benes, E., 23
Beria, L. P., 14, 44, 185, 188
Bierut, B., 15
Brezhnev, L. I., 128, 178, 180ff, 194ff, 208
Bukharin, N. I., 26
Bulgaria, 15, 27, 29, 55, 129, 186, 189

Chervenkov, V., 15
China
  Nixon's visit, 208
  For dispute with USSR, see Sino-Soviet dispute

Chou En-Lai, 112–13
Consumer goods, 10, 35ff, 38ff, 189, 194ff
Council for Mutual Economic Assistance (Comecon), 119, 125ff, 129, 187, 207
Cult of personality, 9, 17, 21, 138, 158
  criticised by Soviet Communist Party, 34; by Khruschev, 45ff; by Gomulka, 78; by Sinyavsky, 143
Czechoslovakia, 10, 35, 55, 151
  collectivisation of agriculture eased, 15, 16
  coup in 1948, 23, 24
  crisis of 1968, 157ff
  economic reform, 129, 136
  riots in Pilsen, 14
  Slansky trial, 27, 30ff
  Warsaw Pact invasion, 175ff

Dahlem, Franz, 28
Daniel, Yuli, 142ff
De-Stalinisation, 10, 128, 138, 148
  in Czechoslovakia, 25, 157
  in Hungary, 57
Dimitrov, Georgi, 28, 29
Djilas, Milovan, 21, 28
Dubcek, Alexander, 158, 159, 171, 172ff, 184, 188
Dulles, John Foster, 55

East Germany, 10, 14, 27, 88, 186, 189
Economic policy, 10, 13
  reforms in Czechoslovakia, 136ff
  reforms in Hungary, 35, 64
  reforms in Russia, 14, 15, 38, 40, 54, 128ff
Eisenhower, Dwight D., 55, 86
Enver, Mamed, 148

Farkas, Mihaly, 63
Fel, Edit, 201ff
Foreign affairs, 17, 40, 42ff, 86ff

Germany, East, see East Germany
Gero, Ernest, 57, 58, 65, 70
Gheorghiu-Dej, Gheorghe, 15, 119, 124
Gierek, Edward, 151, 190ff
Goebbels, Joseph, 193
Gomulka, Wladyslaw, 27, 65, 72, 75, 76ff, 129, 151, 152ff, 157, 189, 190, 191
Gottwald, Klement, 15
Grigorenko, Pyotr, 145ff, 184

Heavy industry, 13, 35, 38, 128
Hofer, Tamas, 201ff
Horthy, Miklos, 135
Hoxha, Enver, 100ff, 108, 112
Hungary, 10, 27, 151, 178, 183, 186
  economic reform, 133ff
  New Course, 15, 16, 35ff
  1956 uprising, 55, 56, 68
Husak, Gustav, 159ff, 188

Intelligentsia, 55
  in Czechoslovakia, 158
  in Poland, 73
  in Soviet Union, 141, 183

Johnson, Lyndon B., 182, 183

Kadar, Janos, 68, 197ff
Kaganovich, Lazar, 14
Kardelj, Edward, 29, 30, 68, 69ff
Khruschev, N. S., passim

Kisielewski, Stefan, 81ff
Kolakowski, Leszek, 73
Kossuth, Louis, 65
Kostov, Traicho, 27
Kosygin, Alexei, 128, 130
Kovacs, Bela, 35
Kovalev, S., 180
Kozlov, Frol, 104
Kuron, Jacek, 149ff

Lebl, Eugene, 32
Lenin, 9, 26, 45ff, 84, 97, 103, 108ff, 118, 121, 126, 131, 138, 179
Liberman, Evsei, 130ff
Liehm, Antonin J., 25

Majerova, Marie, 18
Malenkov, Georgi, 14, 16, 19, 20, 39ff, 42, 58
Mao Tse-Tung, 43, 84ff, 100, 108, 113, 114
Mariassy, Judith, 56
Marx, Karl, 26, 73, 84, 122, 160, 186
Mickiewicz, Adam, 152
Mikoyan, Anastas, 57, 100
Moczar, Mieczyslaw, 152, 154
Modzelewski, Karol, 149ff, 152
Molotov, V. M., 14, 30

Nagy, Imre, 15, 16, 35ff, 58, 62, 63, 65, 67, 68, 71
Nazism, 13, 24, 27, 99, 104, 154
Nixon, Richard M., 208
Novotny, Antonin, 158
Nyers, Rezsoe, 134ff

Ochab, Edward, 72
Osmanov, Savri, 148
Osmanov, Yuri, 148

Palffy, Gyorgy, 58
Patrascanu, Lucretius, 28
Pauker, Anna, 27, 119
Pavlinchuk, Valery, 184
Podgorny, Nikolai, 128

Poland, 10, 23, 183, 186, 187
  agriculture, 15, 16, 200
  anti-semitism, 152ff
  crisis of 1956, 55, 65, 72ff
  crisis of 1968, 148
  crisis of 1970, 188ff
  purges, 27
Purges, 10, 42, 54
  amnesty, 14
  criticised by Khruschev, 45
  executions, 27ff
  in Hungary, 57
  justification of, 19
  of nationalities, 144
  rehabilitations, 64, 159, 161ff
  Slansky trial, 30

Rajk, Laszlo, 27, 58ff
Rakosi, Matyas, 15, 57, 62, 63, 70
Rokossowski, Konstantin, 75
Rostropovich, Mstislav, 188
Rumania, 15, 27, 29, 55, 189
  break with Comecon, 87, 119
Rusk, Dean, 182

Sakharov, Andrei, 183, 188
Shehu, Mehmet, 100
Shelest, Pyotr, 178
Shepilov, Dmitri, 40ff
Sik, Ota, 165ff
Sino-Soviet dispute, 43, 84, 99, 108,
  112ff, 124, 145, 185
Sinyavsky, Andrei, 142ff
Slansky, Rudolf, 27, 30ff
Slepov, 35
Solzhenitsyn, Alexander, 139ff, 144,
  183, 188
Soviet Union, 10, 11, 13, 54, 151,
  189, 208
  economic reform, 38ff, 138
  relations with Albania, 99ff

relations with China, see Sino-
  Soviet dispute
relations with Czechoslovakia,
  182ff, 189
relations with Hungary, 66ff
relations with Poland, 75ff
relations with Rumania, 87, 119
relations with Yugoslavia, 27ff,
  42, 87
Stalin, J. V., passim
Suslov, Mikhail, 57
Szalai, Andras, 58
Szonyi, Tibor, 58

Thorez, Maurice, 102
Tito, Josip, 17, 21, 92, 99, 105
  break with Stalin, 27, 42
  reaction to Hungarian crisis, 68,
    84
  relations with Albania, 28ff, 100
  relations with Khruschev, 43, 56,
    87ff
Titoism, 13, 27, 30, 42, 101, 106
Truman, Harry S., 23, 24

Ulbricht, Walter, 14, 15, 28

Vaculik, Ludvik, 165ff

Werblan, Andrzej, 155ff
Workers' riots
  in Czechoslovakia, 14
  in East Germany, 14
  in Poland, 72, 77, 189ff

Xoxe, Koci, 100

Yakhimovich, 184
Yugoslavia, 13, 17, 27ff, 42, 68,
  87ff, 92ff, 200. See also Tito,
  Josip